W9-CFY-923

READ TO ME

RECOMMENDED LITERATURE FOR CHILDREN AGES TWO THROUGH SEVEN

Prepared under the direction of the
Curriculum, Instruction, and Assessment Division

in cooperation with the
Child Development Division

CALIFORNIA DEPARTMENT OF EDUCATION

PUBLISHING INFORMATION

Read to Me: Recommended Literature for Children Ages Two Through Seven was prepared under the direction of the Department of Education's Curriculum, Instruction, and Assessment Division in cooperation with the Child Development Division. The document was edited for publication by Mirko Strazicich, working in cooperation with Mae Gundlach and assisted by Janet Lundin. It was prepared for photo-offset production by the staff of the Bureau of Publications, with artwork and layout by Cheryl Shawver McDonald. The cover drawing is by Jerry Pinkney. Typesetting was done by Carey Johnson.

The document was published by the California Department of Education, 721 Capitol Mall, Sacramento, California (mailing address: P.O. Box 944272, Sacramento, CA 94244-2720). It was printed by the Office of State Printing and distributed under the provisions of the Library Distribution Act and *Government Code* Section 11096.

Copies of this publication are available for $5.50, each, plus sales tax for California residents, from the Bureau of Publications, Sales Unit, P.O. Box 271, Sacramento, CA 95812-0271 (telephone: 916-445-1260). A complete list of departmental publications can be obtained by contacting the Sales Unit at the address or telephone number listed above.

ISBN 0-8011-1048-3

ABOUT THE COVER

Jerry Pinkney, a nationally renowned illustrator, has been illustrating children's books since 1964. He received the Caldecott Honor Medal award twice, the Coretta Scott King award three times, and numerous other awards. Most recently, in 1992, he was awarded the Drexel Citation for Children's Literature from Drexel University for his extensive body of work.

Jerry Pinkney was born in Philadelphia, Pennsylvania, on December 22, 1939. From an early age he took an interest in drawing. Following his graduation from the commercial art course at Dobbins Vocational School, Mr. Pinkney received a full scholarship to the Philadelphia Museum College of Art. After working a number of years as a designer for other firms, he established his own studio—the Jerry Pinkney Studio.

A dominant theme of Jerry Pinkney's work is his sensitivity to and interest in a variety of cultures. He has drawn inspiration for a significant part of his work from the African-American culture.

The child on the cover of this publication *Read to Me* is his granddaughter Gloria.

CONTENTS

FOREWORD

"R EAD TO ME! READ TO ME! PLEASE READ ME A STORY!" IS A FAMILIAR REFRAIN heard time and again as young children ask to hear a favorite story read aloud. So it is with great pleasure that I present this carefully selected and annotated list of books for young children ages two through seven. This list, to be used by parents, teachers, librarians, and caregivers of children brings together the home, school, and community in the crucial task of developing our children's abilities to read and appreciate good literature. Through this sharing of books, both children and adults gain an image of themselves as readers and writers. Such an image is important in promoting and establishing literacy.

Studies dealing with children who learn to read fluently without formal instruction at home or before instruction begins in school indicate that these early readers are read to aloud on a regular basis and have early and frequent exposure to books, reading, print, and pictures of all kinds. Interacting with books and stories should be an interesting and satisfying experience. Such interaction plays a vital part in the emerging and developing literacy of young children. The stories children hear and the books they see should be full of meaning from the very start so that they can be stimulated to think about what they are hearing and seeing—to react to the stories and illustrations, to get ideas from them, and to link these ideas with other ideas from their memory of other experiences.

Because this early contact with books is so important in a child's development, we in the California Department of Education, with valuable contributions from an advisory committee of educators, have compiled and annotated a list of approximately 400 titles suitable for children two through seven years of age. The titles represent classic and contemporary favorites such as *Goodnight Moon* by Margaret Wise Brown and *Mirandy and Brother Wind* by Patricia McKissack and concept books such as *Here Are My Hands* by Bill Martin, Jr., and *Little Blue and Little Yellow* by Leo Lionni. I recommend the books on this list to you as a start in bringing young children and books together for enjoyment and enrichment.

Bill Honig

State Superintendent of Public Instruction

PREFACE

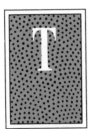
HE BOOKS SELECTED FOR THIS PUBLICATION, *Read to Me: Recommended Literature for Children Ages Two Through Seven,* are for young children who are just beginning the long and arduous yet joyous and rewarding road to achieving full literacy. The titles were carefully selected and annotated by a committee of preschool specialists, teachers, librarians, administrators, and curriculum planners from throughout California. *Read to Me* is specifically intended for adults who know and love children and want to help them grow up "hooked on books." One of the pleasures of being adults who care about children is helping them choose stories to hear and books to read. In his 1982 Caldecott Medal acceptance speech, artist-writer Chris Van Allsburg said, "Children can possess a book in a way they can never possess a video game, a television show, or a Darth Vader doll. . . . A book comes alive when they read it. They give it life themselves by understanding it."

These selections were made to (1) encourage young children to enjoy hearing stories and being introduced to pictures and print; (2) help children view reading as a worthwhile activity; (3) help local curriculum planners select books for their early childhood education programs; (4) assist parents and early child caregivers to make wise choices of enjoyable books for their children; and (5) stimulate educators at the local level to evaluate their literacy development programs and change or improve them, as necessary.

To ensure that *Read to Me* would be of the highest quality, the committee of compilers met for over a year to review and annotate several thousand titles. After many meetings, telephone calls, and exchanges of letters, the members agreed on the 400-plus titles listed in this document. The titles represent classical as well as contemporary picture books, storybooks, and concept books. *Read to Me* includes works in other languages, stories with a multicultural perspective, and books recognized as traditional favorites. These categories are identified in bold print following their respective annotations. A star (★) additionally identifies traditional favorites.

We give special recognition and thanks to Eleanor Clement-Glass, who served with distinction as the chair of the committee. Her organizational skills and untiring efforts enabled the other members to make this document a reality. Another special recognition goes to Armin Schulz for his outstanding work in synthesizing and drafting the final version of each annotation. We are grateful to the educators whose names appear in the Acknowledgments for developing and producing a document that represents such a wide variety of titles in children's literature. In addition, we are grateful to the many educators and parents who made recommendations to committee members as they sought advice from colleagues. Special thanks go to the various child care and development centers throughout the state for their many suggestions.

We are especially grateful to Jerry Pinkney, nationally renowned illustrator, for his donation of the cover artwork. He created the drawing specifically for this publication. We are indeed appreciative of his generosity.

We are pleased to present this first edition of *Read to Me: Recommended Literature for Children Ages Two Through Seven*. It is only a start; we know there are many more favorites that are not listed. We hope to keep this document a living one—one to which new titles will be added in subsequent editions.

SALLY MENTOR
Deputy Superintendent
Curriculum and Instructional
Leadership Branch

FRED TEMPES
Director
Curriculum, Instruction, and
Assessment Division

ROBERT A. CERVANTES
Director
Child Development Division

SHIRLEY HAZLETT
Manager
Language Arts and Foreign
Languages Office

ACKNOWLEDGMENTS

 THIS PUBLICATION OF RECOMMENDED BOOKS FOR THE VERY YOUNG CHILD WAS prepared with the help of an advisory committee composed of early childhood educators, including curriculum planners, consultants, college professors, teachers, and librarians. State Superintendent of Public Instruction Bill Honig and members of his staff are most grateful for the efforts and contributions of the committee members. The members of the committee included the following:

Sandra Balderrama-Escobar, Librarian,
Berkeley Public Library

Genie Barry, Early Childhood Education Consultant,
Oakland

Kathy Buxton, Library Supervisor,
Fair Oaks Branch, Sacramento Public Library

Eleanor Clement-Glass, Education Programs Coordinator,
Beryl Buck Institute for Education, Novato

Catharine Farrell, Private Consultant and Author,
Word Weaving, Inc., Sacramento

Betty Halpern, Early Childhood Education Professor,
Sonoma State University

Kathleen Landon, Library Media Teacher,
Mickey Cox Elementary School, Clovis Unified School District

Donna Matthies, Library Media Teacher,
Willis Jepson Middle School, Vacaville Unified School District

Raquel Mireles, Bilingual Teacher and California Literature Project Teacher Leader,
Furgeson Elementary School, ABC Unified School District

Armin Schulz, Curriculum Coordinator, Sylvan Union Elementary School District; and California Literature Project Director, California State University, Stanislaus

A special thank you is extended to **Eleanor Clement-Glass,** who served as the cochair of the committee and worked with the committee and staff from the Department of Education in the preparation of this document.

The Department of Education's staff members who contributed to the development of this publication were:

Virginia Benson, Consultant, Child Development Division

Mae Gundlach, Consultant, Language Arts and Foreign Languages Office; and Cochair of the Committee

Shirley Hazlett, Manager, Language Arts and Foreign Languages Office

Tomas Lopez, Director, Office of Humanities Curriculum Services

Department of Education staff support was provided by:

Diane Davis, Office of Humanities Curriculum Services

Gerin Pebbles, Language Arts and Foreign Languages Office

Paul Sanchez, Language Arts and Foreign Languages Office

Dolores Vidales, Language Arts and Foreign Languages Office

Linda Vocal, Office of Humanities Curriculum Services

INTRODUCTION

"POETRY MAKES MY HEART GULP," SAID A KINDERGARTEN GIRL, CAPTIVATED by the poetry her teacher had read to the class. Early experiences with literature affect children deeply and powerfully. Something resonates within them as they engage fully in the ideas and language of stories and poems read aloud. Children come to love the world of books with the same enthusiasm that they give to their daily play activities.

The exuberance and enthusiasm of children as they journey through the world of literature is captured by David McCord:

> Books fall open, you fall in,
> Delighted where you've never been;
> Hear voices not once heard before,
> Reach world on world through door on door;
> Find unexpected keys to things
> Locked up beyond imaginings.
> (Excerpt from the poem "Books Fall Open" by David McCord)

We wish for all children, and the adults who love and teach them, the joys of literature that can be found through exploration of the literature suggested in this collection. As in any journey, we know that caring adults are needed to take the first steps with children on the path to reading. In the words of American author Orville Prescott, "Few children learn to love books by themselves. Someone has to lure them into the wonderful world of the written word; someone has to show them the way. . . ."

What is the purpose of the recommended literature list?

The main goal of this publication is to get children hooked on books early in life and to promote the warm, shared reading experiences that will connect adults to children in unique and personal ways. Children should see the love of reading as an end in itself and learn that books can offer deeply moving and fulfilling life experiences, lifelong learning, and personal joy.

The hectic pace of modern living often leaves parents with less time to spend with their young children. How can parents and children make the most of their precious time together? What can parents give their young children that will have lasting value, enrich the quality of the relationship between parent and child, and contribute to children's growth and development?

By reading to children, adults can help them to understand the world and use literature as a springboard for many conversations about feelings, families, and the larger world outside the family. The talking and sharing stimulated by looking at picture books and hearing wonderful stories read aloud have deep value for children. We hope that this collection of books will provide a starting place for adults and the children in their care to begin their journey into the world of literature.

As you share these special read-aloud times with young children, either as a parent, teacher, librarian, or other special adult in the child's life, you are offering a wonderful, powerful gift that will last a lifetime. This collection of titles is intended to be illustrative rather than definitive. This publication could not possibly include all the wonderful contemporary stories or all the time-honored classics. But the committee members have tried to provide a wide selection of authors, illustrators, and topics that will entice and excite young readers from two to seven years of age.

Why is literature important for young children?

Reading and talking about stories, poems, songs, and chants affect the development of young children significantly and occupy a central place in their lives. Children benefit in many different ways:

- Reading stories aloud to children and talking together bond children and adults and play an important role in building positive family relationships.

- Literature helps develop attitudes about life and helps children begin to interpret and make sense of the world around them.

- Reading aloud to children helps to develop future readers. When adults actively model the act of reading, they convey the value they place on reading and the importance of books and stories. Research studies have shown that children who have been read to in early childhood become effective readers and writers in school and lifelong readers as well.

- Reading aloud to children provides for their language development. Children learn about language through its use. Storytelling, both from the oral tradition and from books, allows children to hear the flow and rhythm of language. Talking about stories and listening to responses from children validate their language and show them the worth of what they say.

- Quality literature offers important information to children and shows them that books are resources for gaining knowledge and applying new ideas.

- Stories transmit and validate culture, allowing readers to see themselves and others. Stories help readers to acknowledge, appreciate, and celebrate cultural diversity. Literature can help adults to validate a child's identity and enhance self-esteem. Positive role models help children to reach their full potential.

- Literature helps children participate in higher-order, philosophical thinking. Talking and thinking about stories enhance children's thinking and reasoning powers.

- Hearing literature read aloud validates experiences of children in their world, the issues that concern them, and their feelings.

- Literature helps children learn how to live. Through stories children can learn social teachings and observe cause-and-effect relationships. The actions of a character and their consequences become apparent. Children can learn to explore the qualities of the characters, place value on behavior, and identify virtues.

The value of literature is summarized by author Katherine Paterson: "I learned that reading can be a road to freedom or a key to a secret garden, which, if tended, will transform all life."

How is the book list organized?

The organizational design of the book list reflects the interests, explorations, and concerns of young children. Each category of books reflects the developmental themes that children are dealing with. These themes address the fundamental life concerns of children and match the child's growing interest and curiosity in a widening view of the world.

The first section of the list is titled "The Child." The first series of books, to be shared with infants and toddlers, is for beginning listeners. Books in this first section are typically board books, bright and colorful, with illustrations of everyday items and brief (if any) text. These selections are the beginning steps in sharing books, talking about pictures, and reading simple stories.

The next collection of stories in this first section focuses on the development of the child's identity. Stories included in this section build the self-concept and self-esteem of children by helping them explore personal character traits and human values, nurturing fantasy and imagination, and exploring a range of emotions.

"The Child's Home and Family" section includes books that offer a range of issues regarding family relationships and validate the daily routines and familiar experiences of a young child. Concrete aspects of the child's world, such as concepts about food, clothing, and home and shelter, are provided in this section. Diversity in family traditions and cultural heritage is honored through various illustrative selections.

Books listed in "The Child's Community" draw the child into friendships outside the family and explore relationships and feelings that come into play. These books introduce a range of neighborhood and community experiences, including celebrations, outings, and new encounters.

Finally, in "The Child's World" curiosity about nature is introduced and encouraged through books about the seasons and the weather, plants and animals, environments, and discovery of many of nature's patterns—colors, numbers, sizes, and shapes. The world community is a fitting ending or beginning for a whole new category of the child's growing understanding of the world.

How were the books selected?

The criteria developed by the committee for book selection appear in the Appendix as an aid in determining future selections of literature for young children. Three major areas of consideration guided the work of the committee:

1. Literary qualities of the story
2. Qualities that appeal to a child
3. Educational potential of the book

Literary qualities include the value of the themes or topics presented; the quality of the illustrations and language used; and the literary structure, including plot and characters. Stories must appeal to children and offer opportunities for personal identification with the characters and settings. Also considered were the teaching and learning potential of a book as well as the production and construction of the book itself.

Criteria for selection and inclusion of books on the recommended list were developed by the advisory committee, members of which included school librarians, college professors who specialize in children's literature, preschool teachers, elementary school teachers, early childhood education consultants, California Literature Project participants, and consultants engaged in curriculum development for early childhood education and for English–language arts. Not all books listed in this document contain content that matches all the listed criteria, but each book has been carefully and thoughtfully selected because it illustrates most of the criteria noted in the Appendix.

In selecting books, the committee tried to balance the classics that have become familiar favorites with selections from contemporary literature. Generally, representative books by particular authors were included rather than an exhaustive list of each author's work. A variety of genres are included throughout each category.

Books were selected that would address the interests and fundamental developmental issues of all young children; that would represent authentic life experiences; and that would help children to make sense of their thoughts, feelings, and experiences. Adults should choose reading materials for young children on the basis of the child's interest, attention span, and life experiences and according to the preferences of both the adult and the child.

Multicultural appeal and representation were important. In this regard images of culturally diverse families and children shown in a variety of life circumstances and settings and depicted in respectful, positive, nonbiased ways were of utmost importance. A concerted effort was made to include books available in languages other than English. Aesthetic qualities of the books were also considered. A major focus of any selection is how well the story lends itself to oral presentation by an adult.

The interplay of the child and adult with the book provides the engaging, shared experience. Naturally, one of the most important criteria for the selection of any book is the shared interest, preference, and relevance of a book to the adult and child. We hope that children and adults will select books from this list to listen to and read from according to their own personal, shared interests.

Should young children from ages two through seven be expected to read the words of the stories in this book list?

Not at all. The books selected are meant for adults to show, read, and tell to young children. The list itself is an important commentary about the central place literature plays in children's lives. For children as infants, then as toddlers and preschoolers, and later as kindergartners and students in elementary school, these books are offered to encourage talking together, listening to children's ideas, sharing family stories and feelings, building a repertoire of family favorites, and learning together about one's own and other cultures.

The young child is *not* expected to be able to decode the vocabulary of many of the books in this offering. By listening to adults reading and rereading stories, children learn the cadence and rhythm of language and build the foundation for reading that will transform them into strong, independent readers later. Through the pleasure of shared reading experiences, children develop the desire to read on their own. Expecting children to read at too early an age or to perform a reading task when they are not ready can be an unwarranted burden that may discourage them from wanting to read books as they grow older.

As children learn to read in first and second grades, they may take pride in reading some of their earlier books. Young children, in fact, will pretend to read the stories that they have actually memorized from the repetitive rereadings of favorite stories. This activity leads them to feeling successful about themselves as future readers.

What is meant by the adult-child shared reading experience?

From infancy, children enjoy the sound of the adults closest to them. They look forward to talking together, listening to family stories about various relatives, or discussing significant family events. Even small, funny incidents make engaging stories that may not seem like literature; but these stories build a strong sense of the family's shared heritage and life together. Family photograph albums often are a child's first book, as stories explaining the pictures flow from page to page while family members look at the album together.

Reading stories aloud to young children is the continuation of the shared family stories. Adults reading to young children from infancy and throughout their early years is a wonderful tradition that enhances and supports the child's development and joy of reading. Many families continue a shared reading time even when the children learn to read. Just as children understand much more than they can express verbally, they understand more of the stories read aloud than they can read for themselves. Hearing stories that are beyond their own level of reading offers a rich language model and food for thought beyond what they could attain with their own limited reading ability.

"The time to read is anytime; no appointment is necessary," says Holbrook Jackson, an English writer. Infants and toddlers, the youngest beginning listeners, love to sit on adult laps, pat pictures, and delight in different items on a picture book page being pointed out by an adult. And first graders sit entranced at circle time listening to Ira's problems in *Ira Sleeps Over*. For all these children the committee members hope that reading and talking about books become an integral part of their daily lives.

Shared reading can occur as part of a regular bedtime or naptime routine, with a parent or older child reading stories to the youngest family members. Books can also offer a prelude or follow-up to an experience of the family or in the classroom. For example, stories about a new baby in the family, such as *A Baby Sister for Frances* or *Here She Comes Bringin' That Little Baby Girl* by John Steptoe, might provide an opening for discussion after the birth of a new baby. Or a reading of *Mike Mulligan's Steam Shovel* might precede a walking field trip to a nearby construction site. Books may be read with one child or a small group or a large group for older children. A favorite neighborhood time could be to have one neighbor read stories each day at 4 p.m. to the children of several families. Children congregate readily to share the enchanting tales and illustrations.

Commercially available books and books that children or families make themselves are worth reading aloud. Because young children consider pictures and illustrations important, adult readers need to show pictures and allow children to study them by touching and talking about them. Having the book available before and after reading the story helps children to anticipate a story or review their favorite parts. Readers should preview the story by asking questions such as, "What do you think the story is about?" or simply stating some relevant tie to the story, such as, "Remember when we saw that long freight train crossing the tracks and we waited a long, long time for it to pass? Well, this story is about a train just like that."

Any story can be made more interesting by animation of voice or facial expressions. Children read an adult's body language and voice and interpret the story as it is shared with them. Sometimes using a puppet or stuffed animal to tell the story or simple props such as three bowls and spoons of varying sizes when *The Three Bears* is being read can help children visualize ideas presented in the story.

Children love to have stories read over and over again. As they become more familiar with the story, they can help tell it with prompts such as, "And then what did she do?" Or one may pause and let the children finish a common refrain of the story, participating in the telling. Young children become excited about being able to move during the story and acting out a sound or movement such as eating porridge with the Three Bears or huffing and puffing along with the Big Bad Wolf.

Sometimes children enjoy talking about different ideas and pictures and relating stories and feelings from their own experiences. Sometimes they enjoy stopping the story to think what might come next or to answer a question about a character or the story. But sometimes too many interruptions can interfere with the sheer enjoyment of the story. A straight reading allows children to gain the full effect of the story and stay entranced in the world created by the language and the tale. Adult readers do not need always to explain and teach a book. The story itself speaks to children, and they should be allowed to listen with undivided attention, allowing their imaginations to reign freely.

Where can the books on this recommended literature list be found?

All of the titles on this recommended list are currently in print and should be available at local public and school libraries as well as at bookstores that have wide offerings of books for young children. Often, good books can be found through neighborhood garage sales or flea markets, book fairs, or book clubs.

Listed books may also be specially ordered from publishers listed in this document. Some of the multilingual and multicultural books, which offer a variety of sources for culturally and linguistically diverse educational materials, can be ordered from sources listed under "Resources for Publications and Instructional Materials."

An important consideration by the committee when making selections was to ensure that the books in this listing would be currently available and easily accessible to a wide range of audiences, from parents and grandparents to teachers and librarians. We encourage families and classroom teachers to expand and elaborate on their own collection of favorites.

Any book list should be a living document that is fluid and dynamic. Users of the list are encouraged to go beyond this illustrative, beginning list, expanding and elaborating on their current collections.

I THE CHILD

At the Beginning: Beginning Listeners

Allen, Pamela. *Fancy That!* Orchard, 1988.

When a brown hen's egg begins to hatch, everyone around has something to say. This familiar story line is told with humor and playful language.

Baer, Gene. *Thump, Thump, Rat-a-Tat-Tat.* Illustrated by Lois Ehlert. Harper Junior, 1989.

The listener is greeted by a marching band unloading from a bus as the story starts. The band then parades across the wildly colorful pages, becoming louder as it gets nearer and softer as it retreats to board the bus for the trip back home.

Browne, Anthony. *Things I Like.* Knopf, 1989.

In this simple tale with its uncluttered text, a small chimpanzee enjoys activities such as hiding, acrobatics, building sand castles, and being with friends. We share in the obvious pleasure of the young chimp as he experiences the world around him. Other books by Browne include *Gorilla, Willy the Champ,* and *Willy the Wimp.*

Bucknall, Caroline. *One Bear All Alone: A Counting Book.* Dial Books, 1986.

This counting book features rhymed couplets that describe all sorts of bear antics starting with one bear all alone, sitting by the telephone, to six bears at the shops buying lots of lollipops. Bucknall's other book, *One Bear in the Picture,* deals with Ted Bear's special day at school—picture day!

Burningham, John. *El Bebe.* Editorial Patria, 1984.

This book, available in both Spanish and English, focuses on learning about being a baby and being a member of a family. Six other books in this toddler series include *El Amigo, El Conejo, El Perro, La Alacena, La Cobija,* and *La Escuela.*

SPANISH

Burningham, John. *Mr. Gumpy's Outing.* Holt, 1971.

When Mr. Gumpy takes a boat ride on the river, his little boat becomes more like an ark. Soon the boat is filled with goats, cats, sheep, dogs, chickens, pigs, and children. When a squabble begins, everyone gets wet! A companion story is *Mr. Gumpy's Motor Car.*

Butterworth, Nick. *Just Like Jasper!* Illustrated by Mick Inkpen. Little, 1989.

Jasper, a black-and-white cat, has some birthday money. He cannot wait to go to the toy store to pick out his own present. The cartoonlike illustrations and the bold, readable print make this an enjoyable experience. Companion books include *Nice or Nasty* (a word concept book) and *One Bear at Bedtime* (a counting book).

Carlstrom, Nancy White. *Jesse Bear, What Will You Wear?* Illustrated by Bruce Degen. Macmillan, 1986.

Jesse Bear, what will you wear, what will you wear in the morning? When Jesse Bear wakes up, he has to make some decisions about what he is going to wear. The story of his choices is told in simple rhyme.

Chorao, Kay. *The Baby's Lap Book.* Dutton, 1977.

This book has more than 50 traditional nursery rhymes along with the author's soft pencil drawings on pastel pages. Chorao's gentle touch is just right. Another title by Chorao is *The Baby's Bedtime Book.*

Cooney, Barbara, and others. *Tortillitas para Mamá and Other Nursery Rhymes in Spanish and English.* Illustrated by Barbara Cooney. Holt, 1981.

This anthology of Latin American nursery rhymes has unique illustrations. The words of each poem or rhyme are given in both Spanish and English. Some suggestions for finger-play activities are included.

SPANISH

★ De Paola, Tomie. *Tomie de Paola's Mother Goose.* Putnam, 1985.

This collection of Mother Goose rhymes, illustrated by author and illustrator Tomie de Paola, presents the original classic versions of the old rhymes whenever possible. Many of the 200 rhymes include favorite characters such as Jack and Jill and Little Bo Peep; lesser-known rhymes are also included.

De Regniers, Beatrice Schenk, and others. *Sing a Song of Popcorn: Every Child's Book of Poems.* Illustrated by nine Caldecott Medal artists. Scholastic, 1988.

This impressive poetry anthology for children of all ages contains 128 poems. The works are divided into nine sections; each section features a different Caldecott award-winning artist. Cultural diversity is represented in the subject matter, the poets, and the artists. Classical poets and modern poets are represented.

Fox, Mem. *Hattie and the Fox.* Illustrated by Patricia Mullins. Bradbury, 1987.

When Hattie Hen warns the rest of the barnyard animals about the danger (a fox) she spies in the bush, they do not pay any attention. The repetitive nature of the book's structure makes this an excellent choice for early listeners to experience. This book is available in "big book" format. This author's other books include *Koala Lou* and *Possum Magic.*

Hague, Kathleen. *Out of the Nursery, into the Night.* Illustrated by Michael Hague. Holt, 1986.

The incredible dreams of teddy bears take the small child on night journeys where anything is possible. Other books by the Hagues include *Alphabears: An ABC Book* and *The Man Who Kept House.*

★ Hutchins, Pat. *Good-Night, Owl!* Macmillan, 1972.

Owl cannot get to sleep during the day with the bees buzzing, the crows cawing, the starlings chittering, and the jays screaming. This humorous, repetitive tale with predictable phrases has an unpredictable ending. This story is available in "big book" format and in Spanish.

SPANISH

Isadora, Rachel. *I Hear* (and related books in the series). Greenwillow, 1985.

This series of books for toddlers builds on everyday experiences in their environment. In *I Hear*, a toddler responds to things she hears such as the "tick tock" of the clock or the footsteps of her cat. Other books in the series include *I See* and *I Touch*.

Jonas, Ann. *Now We Can Go.* Greenwillow, 1986.

A small child refuses to leave the house until all his treasures are put in his travel bag. Bright colors and clearly defined objects make this a perfect choice for preschoolers.

Krementz, Jill. *Taryn Goes to the Dentist.* Crown, 1986.

By means of photographs in board book format, the author describes a little girl's visit to the dentist.

★ Martin, Jr., Bill. *Brown Bear, Brown Bear, What Do You See?* Illustrated by Eric Carle. Holt, 1967, 1983.

Unique, colorful animals parade across the pages of this "classic" story by Bill Martin, Jr. The repetitive nature of the simple tale is so predictable that children can easily "read" the text from the picture clues provided. This book is a "model" concept book for reinforcing the color words and for creating similar pattern stories.

O'Donnell, Elizabeth. *I Can't Get My Turtle to Move.* Illustrated by Maxie Chambliss. Morrow Junior, 1989.

This story provides an approach to developing number concepts from one to ten. The narrator is able to get all her animal friends active (three kittens purr, four puppies sit, seven ants march, and so on) except the turtle, which will not move. She finally succeeds—with one magic word.

Ormerod, Jan. *Silly Goose.* Lothrop, 1986.

A little girl delights in silliness as she tells all the ways she can move like various animals. This book is part of a series of books about toddlers.

Oxenbury, Helen. *The Checkup.* Dutton, 1983.

This book is one of many board books and picture books by this author. *The Checkup* is a simple story about a young child's visit to the doctor. Oxenbury's talent of revealing the humorous side of everyday life through simple text and funny illustrations is evident in this selection.

Oxenbury, Helen. ***Say Goodnight.*** Macmillan, 1987.

Say Goodnight is one book in a series of large board books with rhyming text and big illustrations for babies and toddlers. The books can be handled easily by toddlers. The books also include a multiethnic variety of babies. Other books in the series include *All Fall Down, Clap Hands,* and *Tickle, Tickle.*

Oxenbury, Helen. ***Tom and Pippo Go for a Walk.*** Macmillan, 1988.

This simple story of taking a walk with a parent illustrates a nurturing relationship between a little boy and his mother. The boy mirrors the security of this relationship with his toy monkey.

Parramón, José María, and J. J. Puig. ***El Gusto.*** Illustrated by María Rius. Barron, 1985.

El Gusto is one of five colorful books that illustrate and describe the five senses. Other books in the series are *El Oido* (hearing), *El Olfato* (smell), *El Tacto* (touch), and *La Vista* (sight). *El Gusto* is about taste.

SPANISH

Pomerantz, Charlotte. ***All Asleep.*** Illustrated by Nancy Tafuri. Penguin, 1986.

This is a soothing bedtime story with Nancy Tafuri's appealing illustrations. Young listeners will enjoy *Early Morning in the Barn* by Tafuri.

Tafuri, Nancy. ***Have You Seen My Duckling?*** Greenwillow, 1984.

When a duckling disappears, a mother duck and her seven other ducklings swim around the pond looking for it. The listener will enjoy finding the duck on each double-page spread. This concept book works as both a counting book and a game book. Another concept book by this author/illustrator is *Who's Counting?*

Teague, Kati. ***Faces.*** Renyl Editions, 1989.

This volume on the uniqueness of faces and people is one of a series of durable, attractive books for beginning listeners. This book has many translations, including Spanish, English, Chinese, and Vietnamese.

CHINESE • SPANISH • VIETNAMESE

Van Laan, Nancy. ***The Big Fat Worm.*** Illustrated by Marisabina Russo. Knopf, 1987.

In this rhythmic read-aloud tale, a chain of events is set in motion when a big fat bird tries to eat a big fat worm.

Watanabe, Shigeo. ***Daddy, Play with Me!*** Illustrated by Yasuo Ohtomo. Putnam, 1986.

Daddy and Baby Bear play horse-and-rider, make a train, and fly a plane until Daddy is exhausted. Then it is nap time for both. This book is part of the I LOVE TO DO THINGS WITH DADDY series, which is popular as story-time reading for the very young child.

> "BEGIN READING TO CHILDREN AS SOON AS POSSIBLE. THE YOUNGER YOU START THEM, THE BETTER."
>
> JIM TRELEASE
> *THE READ-ALOUD HANDBOOK*
> 1984, P. 65

Watanabe, Shigeo. *How Do I Put It On?* Illustrated by Yasuo Ohtomo. Putnam, 1984.

This book is one of a series of books for the very young child about growing up and learning to do things independently. Children identify readily with the little bear. Other books in the series include *I Can Build a House, I Can Take a Walk,* and *I'm the King of the Castle.*

Weiss, Nicki. *Where Does the Brown Bear Go?* Illustrated by Monica Weiss. Greenwillow, 1989.

In this enchanting bedtime poem, all the animals of the world are on their way home, ready to go to bed. The rhythmic pattern of the story-poem is appealing to children.

Wells, Rosemary. *Max's First Word.* Dial Books, 1979.

Young children will enjoy Wells's lovable toddler rabbit, Max, and his extremely talkative sister, Ruby. In this book Max learns to talk. Other books in the series include *Max's New Suit, Max's Ride, Max's Toys: A Counting Book,* and *Say Apple, Max.*

THE MAIN PURPOSE OF THIS PUBLICATION IS TO GET CHILDREN HOOKED ON BOOKS EARLY IN LIFE.

Winter, Paula. *The Bear and the Fly.* Crown, 1976, 1987.

As the wordless story begins, three bears are enjoying dinner. Unfortunately, a fly arrives and begins to bother everybody. Father Bear desperately tries to get rid of the fly and return to his once peaceful meal. Chaos ensues in this hilarious tale.

Yolen, Jane. *The Three Bears Rhyme Book.* Illustrated by Jane Dyer. Harcourt Brace Jovanovich, 1987.

This collection of rhymes and pictures celebrates the everyday life of Goldilocks and the Three Bears. Events in the book are seen through the eyes of Baby Bear. Goldilocks is presented in a positive way. Other books for young listeners by Yolen include *The Girl Who Loved the Wind, The Lullaby Songbook,* and the COMMANDER TOAD series for early readers.

Self-concept and Self-esteem

Alexander, Martha. ***Blackboard Bear.*** Dial Book, 1969.

A child's vivid imagination is shown in this appealing story about being too little to play with the other children. The young lad in the story creates his own friend—a large blackboard bear—who magically comes to life.

Alexander, Martha. ***My Outrageous Friend Charlie.*** Dial Books, 1989.

Jessie Mae admires her outrageous friend Charlie because he can do anything. Charlie keeps telling Jessie Mae that she can be just like him. To help Jessie, Charlie gives her a Super Deluxe Triple Magic kit for her birthday. And in the end Jessie Mae becomes Charlie's "outrageous" friend.

Aliki. ***My Five Senses.*** Harper Junior, 1989.

Aliki develops a child's understanding of the five senses in this "Let's-Read-and-Find-Out" science concept book. Children identify what the senses are and how we learn through them about the world around us.

Allen, Jeffrey. ***Mary Alice, Operator Number 9.*** Illustrated by James Marshall. Little, 1975.

When Mary Alice, the town's expert telephone operator duck, becomes ill, disaster strikes. Mary Alice's boss looks for a replacement, but no other animal can fill her position. The boss humorously learns that Mary Alice is irreplaceable. The sequel to this book is *Mary Alice Returns.*

Baker, Keith. ***The Magic Fan.*** Harcourt Brace Jovanovich, 1989.

Set in Japan, this is a beautiful story about Yoshi, a boy who found a magic fan and discovered that it changed his life forever.

JAPANESE CULTURE

Bemelmans, Ludwig. ***Madeline.*** Viking, 1939, 1985.

Madeline is a nonconformist in a Paris convent school. Told in rhyme, the story of Madeline's appendicitis becomes an adventure. Other titles in this series include *Madeline's Rescue* and *Madeline and the Bad Hat.*

Breinburg, Petronella. ***Shawn Goes to School***. Illustrated by Errol Lloyd. Harper Junior, 1974.

Shawn wants to go to preschool; but the first day is scary, and he cries. Things get better soon, and he begins to enjoy school. The illustrations depict an African-American child.

Brightman, Alan. *Like Me.* Little, 1976.

A child looks at his developmentally delayed friends and decides that everyone is the same but some people are faster and some are slower. Beautiful photographs highlight the text.

Butterworth, Nick. *Just Like Jasper!* Illustrated by Mick Inkpen. Little, 1989.

Jasper, a black-and-white cat, has some birthday money. He cannot wait to go to the toy store to pick out his own present. The cartoonlike illustrations and the bold, readable print make this an enjoyable experience. Companion books include *Nice or Nasty* (a word concept book) and *One Bear at Bedtime* (a counting book).

Carlson, Nancy. *Harriet's Recital.* Carolrhoda, 1982.

Harriet loves to dance, but once a year her ballet class gives a recital. For a week she worries and frets about the event. When the big day arrives, Harriet still insists she cannot perform. With her teacher's support and encouragement, Harriet overcomes her stage fright and begins dancing.

Carlstrom, Nancy White. *Jesse Bear, What Will You Wear?* Illustrated by Bruce Degen. Macmillan, 1986.

Jesse Bear, what will you wear, what will you wear in the morning? When Jesse Bear wakes up, he has to make some decisions about what he is going to wear. The story of his choices is told in simple rhyme.

Demi. *The Empty Pot.* Holt, 1990.

This beautifully illustrated Chinese folktale deals with the themes of honesty and courage. Young Ping is ashamed that his seeds from the emperor will not blossom, but he honestly admits this to the emperor. The emperor rewards Ping's honesty, courage, and worthiness by making him the next emperor. Another beautiful book by Demi is *Liang and the Magic Paintbrush.*

CHINESE CULTURE

De Paola, Tomie. *The Art Lesson.* Putnam, 1989.

Young Tommy knows he wants to be an artist when he grows up. He is excited about going to school and having art lessons but not about the rules in school. When he is encouraged by the art teacher, Tommy realizes his true ambition to be an artist. This autobiographical book is the author's own story.

★ Freeman, Donald. *Dandelion.* Viking, 1964.

When Dandelion receives an invitation to Jennifer Giraffe's tea-and-taffy party, he gets his mane curled and nails manicured; and then he buys a snappy jacket, cap, and walking cane. But Jennifer doesn't recognize him until he gets caught in a cloudburst, loses his hat and curls, and changes back to his "normal" self. Freeman's other books, *Corduroy* and *A Pocket for Corduroy,* are also delightful reading.

★ Galdone, Paul. *The Little Red Hen.* Houghton Mifflin/Clarion, 1973.

This repetitive tale presents the story of the clever little red hen and her three lazy friends. When asked to help with the chores, each friend replies, "Not I." So the little hen teaches them a lesson about helping and cooperating. Other books or retellings by this author include *Jack and the Beanstalk, Puss in Boots, The Teeny-Tiny Woman,* and *The Three Bears.* All of these titles, except *The Teeny-Tiny Woman,* are available in Spanish. Margot Zemach also has a delightful version of *The Little Red Hen.*

SPANISH

Goennel, Heidi. *Sometimes I Like to Be Alone.* Little, 1989.

The author recounts the special things, real and imagined, that a young girl does when alone. These include going fishing, making a card for a special friend, or pretending to be in a chorus line. Other books by Goennel include *If I Were a Penguin . . . , My Day,* and *My Dog.*

Goennel, Heidi. *When I Grow Up . . . .* Little, 1987.

Every child dreams of doing grown-up things—driving a car, shaving, dancing in a ballet, or building a house. In this colorful book the author/illustrator presents her own view of all the wonderful things we look forward to doing when we are grown up.

Hughes, Shirley. *Alfie's Feet.* Lothrop, 1982.

Alfie is a young boy with an even younger sister, Annie Rose. In this book Alfie shows all sorts of things he likes to do with feet, from counting Annie Rose's "piggies" to splashing in puddles. Other titles in the ALFIE series include *The Alfie and Annie Rose Storybook, Alfie Gets in First, Alfie Gives a Hand,* and *An Evening at Alfie's.*

Hutchins, Pat. *Happy Birthday, Sam.* Greenwillow, 1978.

It is Sam's birthday. He is a whole year older but not much bigger. He still cannot reach the light switch or his clothes in the closet or the taps on the sink in the bathroom. But Grandpa sends him a little chair "just the right size" that allows him to solve all those problems.

Jensen, Virginia Allen. *Sara and the Door.* Illustrated by Ann Strugnell. Lippincott, 1977.

Three-year-old Sara accidentally shuts the door on her coat. The doorknob is too high, the coat is too tightly wedged, and other people are out of hearing range. How Sara solves the problem makes for a satisfying conclusion.

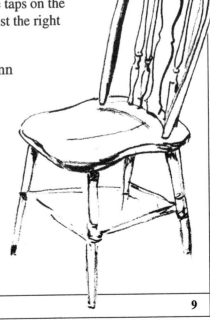

Kraus, Robert. *Leo the Late Bloomer.* Illustrated by José Aruego. Harper Junior, 1987.

Leo, a young tiger, cannot do anything right. He cannot read or write, and he is very sloppy. His father is concerned, but his mother says, "He's just a late bloomer." Leo's father watches and watches until he forgets to watch any longer. And then one day—Leo blooms! This book is available in a Spanish translation.

SPANISH

Levine, Ellen. *I Hate English!* Illustrated by Steve Bjorkman. Scholastic, 1989.

A young girl from Hong Kong moves to New York City. She loves her native language and does not want to learn English. With the help of a clever, understanding tutor, Mei Mei learns that she can keep her native language and learn English too!

CHINESE CULTURE

McPhail, David. *Something Special.* Little, 1988.

Sam, the youngest raccoon in the family, realizes that everyone in his family can do "something special." Sam tries to copy them, but without much success. Finally, when watching his mother work, he helps her with a problem and finds his special talent.

Most, Bernard. *The Cow That Went Oink.* Harcourt Brace Jovanovich, 1990.

A cow that oinks and a pig that moos are ridiculed by the other barnyard animals until each teaches the other a new sound.

Ormerod, Jan. *Silly Goose.* Lothrop, 1986.

A little girl delights in silliness as she tells all the ways she can move like various animals. This book is part of a series of books about toddlers.

Paek, Min. *Aekyung's Dream.* Children's Press, 1988.

In this tender story, a little Korean girl struggles to adjust to her new life in America.

KOREAN CULTURE

Samuels, Barbara. *Duncan and Dolores.* Macmillan, 1986.

Four-year-old Dolores wants a pet that she can call her very own. Duncan, a four-year-old feline, is up for adoption. Dolores annoys the poor cat and is rebuffed and ignored repeatedly. Dolores is heartbroken and decides to ignore the cat as he ignored her. Her method works!

Schwartz, Amy. *Annabelle Swift, Kindergartner.* Orchard, 1988.

Annabelle's older sister gives her some hints on how to "do your best" in kindergarten. Unfortunately, her suggestions to her younger sister do not seem to be doing much good. Annabelle's ability to count money, however, saves the day and builds a good feeling about going to kindergarten.

★ Sendak, Maurice. *Where the Wild Things Are.* Harper Junior, 1963, 1988.

When Max is sent to his room and bed without supper, he dreams a strange, glorious dream about meeting the "wild things" and controlling all of their actions. This classic acknowledges the urge for independence that all young children have. Chinese and Spanish translations are available. The Spanish title is *Donde Viven los Monstruos.*

CHINESE • SPANISH

Shannon, George. *Lizard's Song.* Illustrated by José Aruego and Ariane Dewey. Greenwillow, 1981.

When Bear wants something, he takes it, but what Bear really wants is Lizard's song. Lizard is happy to share it, but somehow Bear cannot get the song correct. Bear finally learns to sing his own song in his own way.

Simon, Norman. *All Kinds of Families.* Illustrated by Joe Lasker. Whitman, 1975.

This concept book about families shows the variety of family compositions and patterns. The loving, supportive, sharing nature of family life is portrayed through a simple, direct text. The story text is illustrated with pen-and-ink drawings.

Soya, Kiyoshi. *A House of Leaves.* Illustrated by Akiko Hayashi. Putnam, 1987.

When caught in a rain shower, young Sarah finds shelter under some leaves. She is joined by a number of small creatures. They all happily share the house of leaves. The illustrator, Akiko Hayashi, has collaborated with author Yoriko Tsutsui to produce several other delightful books: *Anna in Charge, Anna's Secret Friend, Anna's Special Present,* and *Before the Picnic.*

Stinson, Kathy. *Red Is Best.* Illustrated by Robin Baird Lewis. Firefly, 1982.

The young narrator of this book has one message, "Red is best!" Her red boots are best because she can take bigger steps; her red mittens are best because she can make better snowballs; and when she paints, painting with red makes her heart sing. This is a delightful adventure with color, envisioned through a young girl's wonderful imagination. It is available in "big book" format and in Spanish as *El Rojo Es el Mejor.*

SPANISH

Waddell, Martin. *Alice the Artist.* Illustrated by Jonathan Langley. Dutton, 1988.

Alice is a young artist who has an idea for a picture. She paints her picture and admits that she really likes it. Her friends offer suggestions about making the picture better. Alice adds all their suggestions, but when a unique critic tells her the picture is not any good, Alice decides that it is best to paint a picture her own way.

Watanabe, Shigeo. *Daddy, Play with Me!* Illustrated by Yasuo Ohtomo. Putnam, 1986.

Daddy and Baby Bear play horse-and-rider, make a train, and fly a plane until Daddy is exhausted. Then it is nap time for both. This book is part of the I LOVE TO DO THINGS WITH DADDY series, which is popular as story-time reading for the very young child.

Watanabe, Shigeo. *How Do I Put It On?* Illustrated by Yasuo Ohtomo. Putnam, 1984.

This book is one of a series of books for the very young child about growing up and learning to do things independently. Children identify readily with the little bear. Other books in the series include *I Can Build a House, I Can Take a Walk,* and *I'm the King of the Castle.*

Wilhelm, Hans. *Oh, What a Mess!* Crown, 1988.

Franklin prides himself on being neat and clean. He is ashamed to have friends visit his home, because his family is lazy and the house is an absolute mess. When Franklin wins the art contest at the school, there is no clean place to display his painting until the family springs into action. This book helps children explore personal pride and family bonding. Another popular book by this author is *Let's Be Friends Again!*

PERSONAL CHARACTER TRAITS AND HUMAN VALUES

Allen, Jeffrey. *Mary Alice, Operator Number 9.* Illustrated by James Marshall. Little, 1975.

When Mary Alice, the town's expert telephone operator duck, becomes ill, disaster strikes. Mary Alice's boss looks for a replacement, but no other animal can fill her position. The boss humorously learns that Mary Alice is irreplaceable. The sequel to this book is *Mary Alice Returns.*

Blaustein, Muriel. *Play Ball, Zachary!* Harper Junior, 1988.

Zachary the tiger cub and his dad are good at different things. His dad wants him to play sports, and Zachary wants to read and draw but most of all not to disappoint Dad. Bright, cartoonish drawings illustrate the different kinds of ability.

Crowe, Robert L. *Clyde Monster.* Illustrated by Kay Chorao. Dutton, 1976.

A young monster is afraid of the dark because he believes that someone may be lurking under the bed or in a corner. The text and humorous illustrations will help children deal with their own fears.

Goffstein, M. B. *Goldie the Dollmaker.* Farrar, 1980.

Goldie is an artist who lives alone and makes dolls. She puts great care into each doll that she creates. Although people cannot understand her loving care, they are drawn to the special quality of her dolls.

Grifalconi, Ann. *Darkness and the Butterfly.* Little, 1987.

Small Osa is fearless during the day in the African valley where she lives, but at night she is afraid of the strange and terrifying things that might lie in the dark.

AFRICAN CULTURE

Havill, Juanita. *Jamaica's Find.* Illustrated by Anne Sibley O'Brien. Houghton Mifflin, 1986.

Jamaica finds a stuffed dog at the park, but instead of putting the toy in the lost and found, she takes it home. Feeling uneasy about her actions, she returns the toy the next day. She meets the girl who lost the toy animal. Jamaica learns that the honesty of her actions helps her feel good about herself.

Henkes, Kevin. *Chester's Way.* Greenwillow, 1988.

Chester and Wilson, the very best of friends, do not know what to make of their new neighbor, Lilly, who is independent and has a mind of her own. Eventually, Lilly proves herself, and new bonds of friendship are established. But then Victor moves into the neighborhood. The listener is allowed to resolve this "new" problem and bring the story to another happy conclusion. Other delightful stories by this author include *Jessica; Sheila Rae, the Brave;* and *A Weekend with Wendell.*

Joose, Barbara M. *Mama, Do You Love Me?* Illustrated by Barbara Lavallee. Chronicle Books, 1991.

A child living in the Arctic learns that a mother's love is unconditional. The setting is in northern Alaska; the story is about the Inuits (Eskimos).

ESKIMO CULTURE

Kantrowitz, Mildred. *Willy Bear.* Illustrated by Nancy Winslow Parker. Macmillan, 1976.

Getting ready for bed can be a traumatic event for a child. In this story the young boy transfers all of his uneasiness to his bear, Willy. This allows the boy to offer advice and share some worries and fears (e.g., a night-light). Finally, he brings the bear to bed with him so that Willy won't be quite so lonely.

Kasza, Keiko. *The Wolf's Chicken Stew.* Putnam, 1987.

The wolf in this tale finds the perfect chicken for his chicken stew but decides the stew will be even better if the chicken were a bit fatter. The wolf leaves the chicken all sorts of gourmet delights on her porch. When he claims his "prize," the wolf is surprised by hundreds of small chicks who shower him with kisses and tell him that he is the best cook in the world!

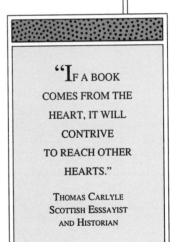

"IF A BOOK COMES FROM THE HEART, IT WILL CONTRIVE TO REACH OTHER HEARTS."

THOMAS CARLYLE
SCOTTISH ESSSAYIST
AND HISTORIAN

Keats, Ezra Jack. **Whistle for Willie.** Penguin, 1964, 1977.

Young Peter wants to be able to whistle more than anything else. He practices and practices, hoping that someday he will be able to whistle for his small dog, Willie. Peter does not give up, and he learns how to whistle.

★ Krauss, Ruth. **The Carrot Seed.** Illustrated by Crockett Johnson. Harper Junior, 1945, 1989.

A little boy plants a carrot seed. He is sure it will come up, but everyone else is sure it will not. Everyday the boy pulls weeds and sprinkles the ground with water. And then one day, the boy's dream is fulfilled, just as he knew it would be. This book is available in Spanish as *Una Semilla de Zanahoria.*

SPANISH

Lewin, Hugh. **Jafta.** Illustrated by Lisa Kopper. Carolrhoda, 1981.

Jafta, a young African boy, compares some of his everyday moods, feelings, and actions with those of the animals that are a common part of his country and his heritage. Young listeners get a wonderful introduction to the use of similes. Other books in the Jafta series include *Jafta and the Wedding, Jafta's Father, Jafta's Mother,* and *Jafta: The Journey.*

AFRICAN CULTURE

Lionni, Leo. **Frederick.** Pantheon, 1967, 1973.

In a family of mice, all except Frederick prepare for winter. He is busy gathering the sun's rays and colors and words. When the food supply runs low during the winter, it is Frederick's turn to share. This book is available in Spanish. Other books by Lionni include *Alexander and the Wind-up Mouse, A Color of His Own, Fish Is Fish, Frederick's Fables, Geraldine the Music Mouse,* and *Let's Make a Rabbit.*

SPANISH

McDermott, Gerald. **Anansi the Spider: A Tale from the Ashanti.** Holt, 1972.

Anansi is a mischief-making spider who falls into many troubles and needs the help of his six children to save him. While trying to reward his sons for their help, Anansi helps put the moon into the sky for all to enjoy. The book is a Caldecott Honor Book depicting the trickster tale from the Ashanti tribe from Ghana.

AFRICAN CULTURE

McKissack, Patricia C. **Flossie and the Fox.** Illustrated by Rachel Isadora. Dial Books, 1986.

Clever, courageous Flossie outsmarts a proud, vain, egg-stealing fox by challenging him to prove that he really is a fox before she will be afraid of him. The text includes African-American dialect from the rural South. McKissack also has written *Mirandy and Brother Wind* and *Nettie Jo's Friends.*

AFRICAN-AMERICAN CULTURE

McPhail, David. *Something Special.* Little, 1988.

Sam, the youngest raccoon in the family, realizes that everyone in his family can do "something special." Sam tries to copy them, but without much success. Finally, when watching his mother work, he helps her with a problem and finds his special talent.

Martinez i Vendrell, María. *La Noche.* Illustrated by Roser Capdevila. Destino, 1986.

Young children will identify with the characters of this story as it treats the fear of the dark in an interesting manner. This book is one of a series called LET'S TALK ABOUT . . . . This book is also available in English/Chinese and English/Vietnamese from Magi Publications, London.

CHINESE • SPANISH • VIETNAMESE

Munsch, Robert N. *The Paper Bag Princess.* Illustrated by Michael Martchenko. Firefly Books, 1980.

Elizabeth, the princess, must outwit the dragon to save Ronald. This is an amusing, nonsexist turnaround of the old "rescue the damsel in distress" tale.

Peet, Bill. *The Kweeks of Kookatumdee.* Houghton Mifflin, 1985.

The birdlike tweeks are starving because their island does not have enough ploppolop fruit trees to feed them all, until Quentin makes an amazing discovery.

★ Piper, Watty. *The Little Engine That Could.* Illustrated by George and Doris Hauman. Putnam, 1930, 1984.

This timeless classic for young listeners is the simple story of the little engine that thought it could help deliver toys and goodies to the children living over the mountain. It is a story of determination and willpower. Even the youngest child will echo, "I think I can . . . I think I can."

Rogers, Jean. *Runaway Mittens.* Illustrated by Rie Munoz. Greenwillow, 1988.

Pica, a young Eskimo boy, has trouble keeping track of the mittens that his grandmother knit for him. After a snowstorm, Pica again looks for his mittens. He finds them in the box where Pin, the sled dog, had her puppies the night before. Pica admits that now his mittens may have a permanent new home.

ESKIMO CULTURE

Samuels, Barbara. *Duncan and Dolores.* Macmillan, 1986.

Four-year-old Dolores wants a pet that she can call her very own. Duncan, a four-year-old feline, is up for adoption. Dolores annoys the poor cat and is rebuffed and ignored repeatedly. Dolores is heartbroken and decides to ignore the cat as he ignored her. Her method works!

Say, Allen. *El Chino.* Houghton Mifflin, 1990.

El Chino is the true story of a Chinese-American youth who becomes a bullfighter in Spain. Vivid, clear watercolors and simple, direct text convey the message that you can be anything you want to be.

Scholes, Katherine. *Peace Begins with You.* Illustrated by Robert Ingpen. Little, 1989.

Differences in philosophy, religion, and feelings are portrayed as elements that often cause gaps of misunderstanding and conflict. This book asks young children to look at peace as something that lives, grows, spreads, and needs to be protected. The hope expressed in the book is that each child can become an important part of creating a peaceful world.

Spier, Peter. *People.* Doubleday, 1980.

Spier's detailed illustrations show many differences among people all over the world. Although over five billion people are living on earth, individual differences make each person unique. This book gently reminds us to appreciate those differences through respect for and tolerance of others.

Steig, William. *Brave Irene.* Farrar, 1986.

In this read-aloud story, Irene struggles through a snowstorm to deliver the duchess' dress that her mother made. Irene meets obstacle after obstacle but finally triumphs and delivers the dress. The author demonstrates an excellent use of language and pictures in wintry colors that get darker as Irene trudges through the snow.

Viorst, Judith. *The Tenth Good Thing About Barney.* Illustrated by Eric Blegvad. Macmillan, 1971, 1987, 1988.

When a pet cat named Barney dies, the young owner tries to deal with his loss and find comfort. He identifies many good things about his cat and, in doing so, eases his pain and builds beautiful memories. This story is suitable for all listeners and readers.

Waddell, Martin. *Alice the Artist.* Illustrated by Jonathan Langley. Dutton, 1988.

Alice is a young artist who has an idea for a picture. She paints a picture and admits that she really likes it. Her friends offer suggestions about making it better. Alice adds all their suggestions, but when a unique critic tells her it is not any good, Alice decides that it is best to paint a picture her own way.

Wolkstein, Diane. *The Banza.* Illustrated by Marc Brown. Dial Books, 1981.

After Teegra, the little tiger, and Cabree, a little goat, are lost and find each other, Teegra's family comes for him. Cabree is lonely until Teegra brings him a banza, an instrument like a banjo, to make music from the heart and keep Cabree safe. This Haitian folktale is perfect for sharing with a group of children.

Wood, Audrey. *Elbert's Bad Word.* Illustrated by Don Wood. Harcourt Brace Jovanovich, 1988.

All children "catch" bad words at some time. The same is true with young Elbert. He snatched them "out of the air" at an elegant garden party and stuffed them into his pocket. The words waited and finally appeared in Elbert's mouth. Then they sprang out, causing a dreadful uproar.

Yolen, Jane. *The Three Bears Rhyme Book.* Illustrated by Jane Dyer. Harcourt Brace Jovanovich, 1987.

This collection of rhymes and pictures celebrates the everyday life of Goldilocks and the Three Bears. Events in the book are seen through the eyes of Baby Bear. Goldilocks is presented in a positive way. Other books for young listeners by Yolen include *The Girl Who Loved the Wind, The Lullaby Songbook,* and the COMMANDER TOAD series for early readers.

Zolotow, Charlotte. *William's Doll.* Illustrated by William Pene Du Bois. Harper Junior, 1972.

Young William wants a doll more than anything. But everyone, except his grandmother, thinks that having a doll will make William a sissy or a creep. In her wisdom she buys William a doll so that he can learn the responsibility of caring for it and gain practice in being a father. Other titles by Zolotow include *I Like to Be Little, If It Weren't for You, My Friend John, The Quarreling Book,* and *The Storm Book.*

PLAYING WITH LANGUAGE

Ada, Alma Flor. *Aserrín, Aserrán.* Illustrated by María del Pilar de Olave. Donars, 1979.

This book contains a short collection of traditional Spanish rhymes, riddles, games, and lullabies.

SPANISH

Ahlberg, Janet and Allan. *Each Peach Pear Plum: An I-Spy Story.* Penguin, 1979, 1986.

This unusual picture book features nursery characters such as Jack and Jill, Little Bo Peep, and others hidden in the illustrations. Children can "spy" them with sharp eyes and might add their own verses to this rhyming story. Another enjoyable book by the Ahlbergs is *The Jolly Postman.*

Baer, Gene. ***Thump, Thump, Rat-a-Tat-Tat.*** Illustrated by Lois Ehlert. Harper Junior, 1989.

The listener is greeted by a marching band unloading from a bus as the story starts. The band then parades across the wildly colorful pages, becoming louder as it gets nearer and softer as it retreats to board the bus for the trip back home. The author and illustrator have created a compelling visual and auditory musical experience.

Bayer, Jane. ***A, My Name Is Alice.*** Illustrated by Steven Kellogg. Dial Books, 1984.

This story introduces the alphabet in a singsong format. Each letter of the alphabet has its own featured page and rhyme.

★ Brown, Margaret Wise. ***Big Red Barn.*** Illustrated by Felicia Bond. Harper Junior, 1989.

This newly illustrated edition of the 1956 rhymed text about farm animals takes the listener through the daily cycle of activities the animals experience. Readers will enjoy the rhymed verse, animal sounds, and reinforcement of color and adjectives. The illustrations depict an African-American family.

Bucknall, Caroline. ***One Bear All Alone: A Counting Book.*** Dial Books, 1986.

This counting book features rhymed couplets that describe all sorts of bear antics starting with one bear all alone, sitting by the telephone, to six bears at the shops buying lots of lollipops. Bucknall's other book, *One Bear in the Picture*, deals with Ted Bear's special day at school—picture day!

Charlip, Remy. ***Fortunately!*** Macmillan, 1964, 1985.

This delightful book is made up of a series of events that have fortunate and unfortunate consequences. Children can easily copy the pattern and write or tell their own "fortunately/unfortunately" stories.

Cooney, Barbara, and others. ***Tortillitas para Mamá and Other Nursery Rhymes in Spanish and English.*** Illustrated by Barbara Cooney. Holt, 1981.

This anthology of Latin American nursery rhymes has unique illustrations. The words of each poem or rhyme are given in both Spanish and English. Some suggestions for finger-play activities are included.

SPANISH

Delacre, Lulu, and Elena Paz. ***Arroz con Leche: Popular Songs and Rhymes from Latin America.*** Illustrated by Lulu Delacre. Scholastic, 1989.

This is a delightful collection of songs, games, and rhymes from Latin American cultures, with rhymes in both Spanish and English. The musical score is found in the back of the book.

SPANISH

Demi. *Opposites: An Animal Game Book.* Grosset, 1987.

Author/illustrator Demi uses members of the animal kingdom to help illustrate the concept of antonyms, or words that are opposite in meaning. Common adjectives (big/little, old/young) are treated most frequently, although there are some prepositions (over/under), a verb or two (come/go), and several nouns (day/night, circle/square). Short verses or riddles accompany each pair of words.

Deming, A. G. *Who Is Tapping at My Window?* Illustrated by Monica Wellington. Dutton, 1988.

Told in simple rhymes, this story attempts to answer the question puzzling a young female character in the story—"Who is tapping at my window?" The listener and reader will meet many animals before they discover that the pitter-patter of the rain is tapping at the window.

★ De Paola, Tomie. *Tomie de Paola's Mother Goose.* Putnam, 1985.

This collection of Mother Goose rhymes, illustrated by author and illustrator Tomie de Paola, presents the original classic versions of the old rhymes whenever possible. Many of the 200 rhymes include favorite characters such as Jack and Jill and Little Bo Peep; lesser-known rhymes are also included.

De Regniers, Beatrice Schenk, and others. *Sing a Song of Popcorn: Every Child's Book of Poems.* Illustrated by nine Caldecott Medal artists. Scholastic, 1988.

This impressive poetry anthology for children of all ages contains 128 poems. The works are divided into nine sections; each section features a different Caldecott award-winning artist. Cultural diversity is represented in the subject matter, the poets, and the artists. Classical poets and modern poets are represented.

★ Emberley, Barbara. *Drummer Hoff.* Illustrated by Ed Emberley. Prentice Hall, 1967.

This Caldecott award-winning classic is a collective tale about young Drummer Hoff, who fires a cannon with the assistance of many other soldiers. Children love the rhyme, repetition, and vivid color designs found in this tale. On the final page, the unused cannon becomes a home for birds and other small animals.

Fox, Mem. *Hattie and the Fox.* Illustrated by Patricia Mullins. Bradbury, 1987.

When Hattie Hen warns the rest of the barnyard animals about the danger (a fox) she spies in the bush, they do not pay any attention. The repetitive nature of the book's structure makes this an excellent choice for early listeners to experience. This book is available in "big book" format. This author's other books include *Koala Lou* and *Possum Magic.*

★ Galdone, Paul. *The Three Little Kittens.* Clarion, 1986.

Three little kittens lose, find, soil, and wash their mittens. This favorite Mother Goose rhyme is about these careless kittens who always manage to correct their mistakes.

Guarino, Deborah. *Is Your Mama a Llama?* Illustrated by Steven Kellogg. Scholastic, 1989.

This book begs to be read aloud as Lloyd, the llama, meets a variety of animals and inquires whether their mamas are llamas. After each animal's mother has been described, the page is turned, and the identity of the animal is revealed.

Hardendorff, Jeanne. *The Bed Just So.* Illustrated by Lisl Weil. Scholastic, 1977.

When a tailor cannot get any sleep, he asks a wise woman for some advice. She tells him that a "hudgin" has come to live with him and the hudgin needs a bed. The tailor has quite a task to find a bed that is neither "too high and too hard" nor "too teeter and too totter."

Hart, Jane. *Singing Bee! A Collection of Favorite Children's Songs.* Illustrated by Anita Lobel. Lothrop, 1982.

This collection of children's songs is arranged by origin, form, seasons, and function. Glorious illustrations accompany the songs.

Heller, Ruth. *A Cache of Jewels and Other Collective Nouns.* Putnam, 1987.

This colorful book about groups of objects or animals introduces young listeners to a wide variety of new vocabulary words through a simple rhyming text. The listener will encounter a "bouquet of flowers" and a "muster of peacocks" as well as a "brood of chicks" and a "clutch of eggs."

Hoguet, Susan Ramsey. *I Unpacked My Grandmother's Trunk.* Dutton, 1983.

This delightful story is built on the following sentence frame: "I unpacked grandmother's trunk and out of it I took . . . ." Twenty-six wonderfully improbable objects are unpacked. This alphabet adventure for preschoolers can easily be a memory game for older children.

Hopkins, Lee Bennett. *Side by Side: Poems to Read Together.* Illustrated by Hilary Knight. Simon and Schuster, 1988.

This is a collection of poems especially chosen to be read aloud. The poems were selected from classic favorites, including poems by Lewis Carroll and Robert Louis Stevenson, and from works of talented contemporary poets, such as Gwendolyn Brooks and David McCord.

★ Hutchins, Pat. *Good-Night, Owl!* Macmillan, 1972.

Owl cannot get to sleep during the day with the bees buzzing, the crows cawing, the starlings chittering, and the jays screaming. This humorous, repetitive tale with predictable phrases has an unpredictable ending. This story is available in "big book" format and in Spanish.
SPANISH

★ Ivimey, John W. *The Complete Story of the Three Blind Mice.* Illustrated by Paul Galdone. Houghton Mifflin, 1989.

Three small mice in search of fun become hungry, scared, blind, wise, and finally, happy. Inspired by the chilling lines of the original nursery rhyme, Ivimey has expanded the rodents' tale and given it a happy ending.

Krauss, Ruth, and Maurice Sendak. *A Very Special House.* Harper Junior, 1953.

This delightfully silly book for young listeners describes a young boy's ideal but imaginary house. The rhyming text matches the whimsical line drawings. Another book by these authors is *The Growing Story.*

Lewin, Hugh. *Jafta.* Illustrated by Lisa Kopper. Carolrhoda, 1981.

Jafta, a young African boy, compares some of his everyday moods, feelings, and actions with those of the animals that are a common part of his country and his heritage. Young listeners get a wonderful introduction to the use of similes. Other books in the Jafta series include *Jafta and the Wedding, Jafta's Father, Jafta's Mother,* and *Jafta: The Journey.*

AFRICAN CULTURE

Lillegard, Dee. *Sitting in My Box.* Illustrated by Jon Agee. Dutton, 1989.

A small boy sits alone in a large cardboard box. Someone knocks and, one by one, a giraffe, an elephant, a baboon, and others join him. Soon the box is full of animals—and more than enough silliness—until the flea arrives. This book celebrates the inventiveness of imaginative play.

McMillan, Bruce. *One Sun: A Book of Terse Verse.* Holiday, 1990.

A day at the beach is illustrated through "terse verse" (verses made up of one-syllable words that rhyme) and photographs. The listener encounters a wet pet, a snail trail, a neat seat, and a scoop group, to name a few. The main character in the book is a charming Asian/Pacific Islander boy.

McPhail, David. *David McPhail's Animals A to Z.* Scholastic, 1988.

This wordless picture book celebrates a letter of the alphabet on each page. Also included on the page is a beautifully illustrated animal that corresponds with that letter. Young toddlers will enjoy adding their descriptive texts as they "read" the pictures. Other books by McPhail are *Emma's Pet, Great Cat, Pig Pig Goes to Camp,* and *Pig Pig Grows Up.*

Martin, Jr., Bill. *Barn Dance!* Illustrated by John Archambault. Holt, 1986.

Unable to sleep on the night of a full moon, a young boy follows the sound of music across the fields and finds an unusual barn dance in progress. The rhymes dance off the reader's tongue as the eye enjoys the various perspectives and the detail of the illustrations.

★ Martin, Jr., Bill. *Brown Bear, Brown Bear, What Do You See?* Illustrated by Eric Carle. Holt, 1967, 1983.

A variety of unique, colorful animals parade across the pages of this "classic" story by Bill Martin, Jr. The repetitive nature of the simple tale is so predictable that children can easily "read" the text from the picture clues provided. This book is a "model" concept book for reinforcing the color words and for creating similar pattern stories.

Martin, Jr., Bill, and John Archambault. *Chicka Chicka Boom Boom.* Illustrated by Lois Ehlert. Simon and Schuster, 1989.

In jump-rope rhythm, the lower-case letters of the alphabet climb a coconut tree until the overloaded tree tumbles them out. After the capital letters comfort them and set them right, the action begins again.

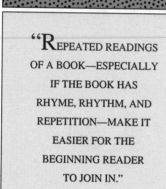

"REPEATED READINGS OF A BOOK—ESPECIALLY IF THE BOOK HAS RHYME, RHYTHM, AND REPETITION—MAKE IT EASIER FOR THE BEGINNING READER TO JOIN IN."

REGIE ROUTMAN
TRANSITIONS: FROM
LITERATURE TO LITERACY
N.D., P. 66

Martin, Jr., Bill, and John Archambault. *Here Are My Hands.* Illustrated by Ted Rand. Holt, 1985.

In this delightful concept book, the young child learns about the various parts of his or her body through rhymed couplets. Children of different ethnic backgrounds are illustrated in Ted Rand's colorful drawings. The book comes to a logical closure with "And here is my skin that bundles me in."

Marzollo, Jean. *Pretend You're a Cat.* Illustrated by Jerry Pinkney. Dial Books, 1990.

This book's rhyming verses ask the reader to purr like a cat, scratch like a dog, leap like a squirrel, and bark like a seal.

Merriam, Eve. *Blackberry Ink.* Illustrated by Hans Wilhelm. Morrow, 1985.

The illustrations are delightful in this collection of humorous and nonsense verses on various themes in a child's world.

Merriam, Eve. *Where Is Everybody? An Animal Alphabet.* Illustrated by Diane de Groat. Simon and Schuster, 1989.

This alphabet book has a variety of animals performing everyday activities of humans. Each page is filled with objects that begin with the featured letter. An additional, humorous touch to each page is having the child locate the animal photographer, a mysterious mole that appears throughout the book.

Merriam, Eve. *You Be Good and I'll Be Night: Jump-on-the-Bed Poems.* Illustrated by Karen Lee Schmidt. Morrow Junior, 1988.

This collection of poems can be used with small toddlers as lap "bounces," lap "jogs," or read-alouds. Older primary children will enjoy them as read-alongs after they have heard them a few times.

Peek, Merle. *Mary Wore Her Red Dress, and Henry Wore His Green Sneakers*. Clarion, 1985, 1988.

Each of Katy Bear's animal friends wears a different color of clothing to her birthday party. The illustrations are colorful.

★ *The Real Mother Goose*. Illustrated by Blanche Fisher Wright. Macmillan, 1916.

The nursery rhymes of Mother Goose are depicted in this early version, a popular one with children, parents, and teachers. Other editions include *Tomie de Paola's Mother Goose*, Michael Hague's *Mother Goose: A Collection of Classic Nursery Rhymes*, *Chinese Mother Goose Rhymes* by Robert Wyndham and Ed Young, and a "big book" version of *Mother Goose*.

Shannon, George. *Dance Away!* Illustrated by José Aruego and Ariane Dewey. Greenwillow, 1982.

Rabbit loves to dance all night and day. He always insists that his friends dance with him. They get tired of dancing with Rabbit until, one day, Fox comes along. Rabbit is able to rescue everyone with his dancing.

Shaw, Nancy. *Sheep in a Jeep*. Houghton Mifflin, 1986.

One bright, sunny day a flock of sheep set off for an excursion in a Jeep. But what a ride they have! The rhythmic text and humorous illustrations will delight even the most reluctant toddler in this short adventure story. Listeners will also enjoy *Sheep on a Ship* by this author.

This Old Man. Illustrated by Carol Jones. Houghton Mifflin, 1990.

Artist Carol Jones has turned this favorite old song into a beautifully illustrated guessing game for young children. The child looks through the peephole and guesses which object is played on next.

Westcott, Nadine Bernard. *The Lady with the Alligator Purse*. Little, 1988.

This well-known rhyme tells the tale of the lively little boy who tries to eat the bathtub. The doctor, the nurse, and the lady with the alligator purse are called in to diagnose the small boy's ailment. The illustrations are zany and appealing!

Williams, Sue. *I Went Walking*. Illustrated by Julie Vivas. Harcourt Brace Jovanovich, 1989.

When a young boy takes a walk, he encounters many colorful animals along the way. They join his excursion in this repetitive, rhythmic text. Julie Vivas's beautiful watercolor illustrations add a very special touch to the book.

Wilner, Isabel. *A Garden Alphabet*. Illustrated by Ashley Wolff. Dutton, 1991.

In rhyming verse this alphabet book describes the variety of activities involved with planning and planting a garden. Young readers will expand their knowledge of garden tools and tasks as well as friendly and unfriendly garden animals. Ashley Wolff's drawings add extra enjoyment to the book.

Winthrop, Elizabeth. *Shoes.* Illustrated by William Joyce. Harper Junior, 1986.

All types of shoes are described in this book told in rhymed verse. The illustrations add extra meaning and humor to the verse. As the book says, we have "shoes with ribbons, shoes with bows, shoes to skate in when it snows."

Wood, Audrey. *The Napping House.* Illustrated by Don Wood. Harcourt Brace Jovanovich, 1984.

In this cumulative tale, everyone is peaceful and sleeping until a wakeful flea on a slumbering mouse starts quite a commotion. The rhyme and rhythm of the tale will capture children's attention and make them want to hear the story over and over again. A sound recording is available.

FANTASY AND IMAGINATION

Alexander, Martha. *Blackboard Bear.* Dial Book, 1969.

A child's vivid imagination is shown in this appealing story about being "too little" to play with the other children. The young lad in the story creates his own friend—a large blackboard bear—who magically comes to life.

Alexander, Martha. *My Outrageous Friend Charlie.* Dial Books, 1989.

Jessie Mae admires her outrageous friend Charlie because he can do anything. Charlie keeps telling Jessie Mae that she can be just like him. To help Jessie, Charlie gives her a Super Deluxe Triple Magic kit for her birthday. And in the end Jessie Mae becomes Charlie's "outrageous" friend.

Arnold, Tedd. *No Jumping on the Bed!* Dial Books, 1987.

Even though he has been warned many times by his father, a young boy continues to jump on his bed. Finally, the bed crashes through several floors and keeps going down toward the basement of his apartment building.

Asch, Frank. *Bear Shadow.* Prentice Hall, 1985.

Frank Asch has found a successful formula for young listeners in his lovable character, Bear, and his unusual adventures. In this book Bear's shadow keeps getting in his way. Bear tries everything possible to get rid of the pest and makes a special deal with his shadow. Other companion books are Asch's *Bear's Bargain, Mooncake, Moongame,* and *Skyfire.*

Asch, Frank. *Happy Birthday, Moon.* Prentice Hall, 1982.

Bear discovers that he and the moon have a birthday on the same day. He decides to give the moon a present—a very special top hat—because that is what he would like also. The ideas of sharing and friendship surface throughout the story as Bear plans his special surprise for the moon.

Berger, Barbara. *Grandfather Twilight.* Putnam, 1986.

At day's end, Grandfather Twilight performs his evening task, bringing the miracle of night to the world. Soothing, luminous, incredible illustrations captivate the eye in this memorable book. Another title by Berger about an imaginary friend is *When the Sun Rose.*

Blocksma, Mary. *Todos Mis Juguetes.* Illustrated by Sandra Cox Kalthoff. Children's Press, 1986.

In a beautiful and playful language, this story tells what happens to toys when they are put away at night. This is a translation of *All My Toys.*

SPANISH

★ Brown, Margaret Wise. *Goodnight Moon.* Illustrated by Clement Hurd. Harper Junior, 1947, 1977.

A young rabbit bids "goodnight" to the familiar objects that can be found in his bedroom. The simple rhymes and illustrations capture a sense of cozy comfort. This book is also available in Spanish as *Buenas Noches Luna.*

SPANISH

Burningham, John. *Would You Rather . . . ?* Harper Junior, 1978.

This book offers a delightful array of choices for the reader and listener from fanciful to scary. Other books by Burningham include *The Blanket, The Friend,* and *Granpa.*

Cooney, Nancy Evans. *The Umbrella Day.* Illustrated by Melissa Bay Mathis. Putnam, 1989.

In this fanciful story, young Missy, wearing a bright yellow slicker and scarlet boots and carrying an old black umbrella, starts out in the rain. When it begins to rain harder, Missy starts wishing. The old umbrella becomes all sorts of imaginative things: a toadstool, a wild-animal tent, and even a boat.

★ De Paola, Tomie. *Tomie de Paola's Mother Goose.* Putnam, 1985.

This collection of Mother Goose rhymes, illustrated by author and illustrator Tomie de Paola, presents the original classic versions of the old rhymes whenever possible. Many of the 200 rhymes include favorite characters such as Jack and Jill and Little Bo Peep; lesser-known rhymes are also included.

★ De Regniers, Beatrice Schenk, and Irene Haas. *A Little House of Your Own.* Illustrated by Irene Haas. Harcourt Brace Jovanovich, 1955.

The author describes the many hideaways and secret nooks that filled her life as a child. Each of these places—from a cardboard box to a treehouse—is explained with detail and special joy.

★ Duvoisin, Roger. *Petunia.* Knopf, 1950, 1989.

Petunia, a silly yet lovable goose, feels that by carrying a book around with her and loving it, she will become wise. With great humor, the author describes "pride without wisdom." This story is considered a children's classic. Another book about Petunia and her friends is *Petunia, I Love You.*

Ets, Marie Hall. *In the Forest.* Viking, 1976.

This repetitive, cumulative tale is about a small boy who goes on a parade into the forest with his paper hat and his new horn. Joining him on this adventure are a group of imaginary animals. Children will enjoy the rhythmic language of the story. Other notable books by Ets include *Just Me* and *Play with Me.*

★ Galdone, Paul. *The Gingerbread Boy.* Clarion, 1975.

This classic tale is about the gingerbread cookie that comes to life and runs away through the countryside encountering animals and people. Gingerbread Boy announces to all that they can't catch him. But then he meets a clever fox. This title is available in Spanish as *El Hombrecito de Pan Jengibre.*

SPANISH

Goennel, Heidi. *When I Grow Up . . . .* Little, 1987.

Every child dreams of doing grown-up things—driving a car, traveling to faraway places, shaving, playing in the World Series, dancing in a ballet, or building a house. In this inviting and colorful book, the author/illustrator presents her own view of all the wonderful things we look forward to doing when we are grown up.

Goode, Diane. *I Hear a Noise.* Dutton, 1988.

A little boy, hearing noises at his window at bedtime, calls for his mother. His worst fears are realized, but he learns that monsters have mothers too.

Graham, John. *I Love You, Mouse.* Illustrated by Tomie de Paola. Harcourt Brace Jovanovich, 1976.

In this short, soothing book, a small child reflects on the things that he would do for the animals he loves if he were one of them. The "pattern" aspect of the words allows the child to predict and "read" along. It is a charming and appealing tale.

Hague, Kathleen. *Out of the Nursery, into the Night.* Illustrated by Michael Hague. Holt, 1986.

The incredible dreams of teddy bears take the small child on night journeys where anything is possible. Other books by the Hagues include *Alphabears: An ABC Book* and *The Man Who Kept House.*

Hogrogrian, Nonny. *One Fine Day.* Macmillan, 1971.

In this cumulative folktale from Armenia, a sly fox steals milk from an old woman, and she cuts off his tail. In order to get the tail back, the fox must complete a series of tasks.

Hoguet, Susan Ramsey. *I Unpacked My Grandmother's Trunk.* Dutton, 1983.

This delightful story is built on the following sentence frame: "I unpacked grandmother's trunk and out of it I took . . . ." Twenty-six wonderfully improbable objects are unpacked. This alphabet adventure for preschoolers can easily be a memory game for older children.

Hutchins, Pat. *Changes, Changes.* Macmillan, 1971.

With a set of colored wooden blocks and a pair of wooden people, Hutchins presents a wordless tale of how the two characters meet a stream of catastrophes with the resources at hand.

★ Hutchins, Pat. *Rosie's Walk.* Macmillan, 1971.

Rosie, the hen, goes for a walk around the barnyard unaware that a fox is following her everywhere. Unfortunately for him, the fox meets with all sorts of obstacles. Children will develop an understanding of word sequences through this amusing animal story. Other books by Hutchins include *Changes, Changes; Don't Forget the Bacon! One Hunter;* and *The Wind Blew.*

★ Ipcar, Dahlov. *The Calico Jungle.* Knopf, 1965.

As part of a bedtime ritual, a young boy traces an imaginary journey among the appliquéd animals on his quilt. When the trip has ended, the animals and the boy are asleep.

Jonas, Ann. *The Trek.* Greenwillow, 1985.

The young narrator encounters all sorts of imaginary wild animals on her daily "trek" to school. Joined on the trek by her helper, another student, they make their way through the desert, over the river, and up the mountain to the school doors—thankful, once again, that they made it! Jonas conceals animals in the everyday things that a child might see on the way to school.

★ Kennedy, Jimmy. *The Teddy Bears' Picnic.* Illustrated by Alexandra Day. Green Tiger, 1983.

This enchanting picture book is based on an old song that was copyrighted in 1907. The bears put on their costumes and have a very special picnic in the woods. Some editions have a recording of the song by Bing Crosby in the back of the book.

Lester, Alison. *Clive Eats Alligators*. Houghton Mifflin, 1985.

In this story seven children make outlandish choices about meals, clothing, occupations, and pets. This book is part of a series that follows these children. Another book in the series is *Rosie Sips Spiders*.

Lillegard, Dee. *Sitting in My Box*. Illustrated by Jon Agee. Dutton, 1989.

A small boy sits alone in a large cardboard box. Someone knocks and, one by one, a giraffe, an elephant, a baboon, and others join him. Soon the box is full of animals—and more than enough silliness—until the flea arrives. This book celebrates the inventiveness of imaginative play.

McMillan, Bruce. *The Remarkable Riderless Runaway Tricycle*. Houghton Mifflin, 1978.

A thrown-away tricycle is returned to its owner, a small boy named Jason. An excellent film is available.

CHILDREN OFTEN LOVE TO HEAR FAMILIAR STORIES READ AGAIN AND AGAIN. REPETITION IS AN IMPORTANT FIRST STEP IN DEVELOPING LITERACY.

★ Marshall, James. *Goldilocks and the Three Bears*. Dial Books, 1988.

In this version of *Goldilocks and the Three Bears*, the listener meets a most unusual bear family. When Goldilocks is discovered, she makes a fast escape and is never seen again by the bears, much to their relief! This story is available in a Spanish version by Maria Claret, *Los Tres Osos*. Jan Brett, Lorinda Cauley, Paul Galdone, and Janet Stevens offer additional English versions.

SPANISH

★ Marshall, James. *Red Riding Hood*. Dial Books, 1987.

This cartoonlike version of the famous old German fairy tale is filled with many humorous moments and interpretations. James Marshall has published other fairy-tale renditions: *Cinderella, Goldilocks and the Three Bears, Hansel and Gretel*, and *The Three Little Pigs*. *Cinderella* is retold by Barbara Karlin and illustrated by Marshall. Other versions of *Little Red Riding Hood* have been retold and illustrated by Paul Galdone, Trina Schart Hyman, Beatrice Schenk de Regniers, and Karen Schmidt. Several versions are available in Spanish.

SPANISH

★ Marshall, James. *The Three Little Pigs.* Dial Books, 1989.

The reader encounters a dressed-up version of the old tale about the pig brothers and their wisdom and folly. The cartoonlike illustrations add additional humor to the text. A Spanish version of this story is available.

Martin, Jr., Bill. *Barn Dance!* Illustrated by John Archambault. Holt, 1986.

Unable to sleep on the night of a full moon, a young boy follows the sound of music across the fields and finds an unusual barn dance in progress. The rhymes dance off the reader's tongue as the eye enjoys the various perspectives and the detail of the illustrations.

Mosel, Arlene. *The Funny Little Woman.* Illustrated by Blair Lent. Dutton, 1972.

In this Japanese tale, a funny little woman who loves to laugh chases her runaway dumpling down a hole. She finds herself on an unusual road and must outwit the three-eyed oni in order to return to her home. Variations to this story can be found in *The Teeny-Tiny Woman* by Tomie de Paola, Paul Galdone, and Jane O'Conner.

JAPANESE CULTURE

Ringgold, Faith. *Tar Beach.* Crown, 1991.

Based on a "quilt painting," *Tar Beach* is the dream story of a young girl as she imagines flying over the city where she and her family live. Her dream allows her to be in charge of her world and to transform it. An African-American family is depicted.

★ Sendak, Maurice. *Where the Wild Things Are.* Illustrated by Maurice Sendak. Harper Junior, 1963, 1988.

When Max is sent to his room and bed without supper, he dreams a strange, glorious dream about meeting the "wild things" and controlling all of their actions. This classic acknowledges the urge for independence that all young children have. Chinese and Spanish translations are available. The Spanish title is *Donde Viven los Monstruos.*

CHINESE • SPANISH

Shannon, George. *Lizard's Song.* Illustrated by José Aruego and Ariane Dewey. Greenwillow, 1981.

When Bear wants something, he takes it, but what Bear really wants is Lizard's song. Lizard is happy to share it, but somehow Bear cannot get the song correct. Bear finally learns to sing his own song in his own way.

Shulevitz, Uri. *One Monday Morning.* Macmillan, 1967.

This cumulative tale, which is based on French folklore, is the story of a king and his court who come to visit a young boy who lives in a rundown apartment building. Unfortunately, the boy is not home during the week to greet them. On Sunday they find him at home and "just drop in to say hello."

★ Slobodkina, Esphyr. *Caps for Sale.* Harper Junior, 1947.

In this children's classic, a tired peddler loses his caps to a treeful of mischievous monkeys. The monkeys eventually return the peddler's caps by imitating his actions. An updated version of this tale is *Fifty Red Night-Caps* by Inga Moore.

★ Stevens, Janet. *Goldilocks and the Three Bears.* Holiday, 1986.

In this upbeat, modernized version of the old tale about Goldilocks, Papa Bear appears in hiking boots, Mama Bear wears high heels, and Baby Bear wears tennis shoes. A Spanish version of this tale, *Los Tres Osos* by Maria Claret, is available. Other popular versions of the tale are written by Jan Brett, Lorinda Bryan Cauley, Paul Galdone, and James Marshall.
SPANISH

★ Stevens, Janet. *The Three Billy Goats Gruff.* Harcourt Brace Jovanovich, 1987.

The author presents an amusing modern-day interpretation of the three billy goats' conflict with the troll. The plan to trick the troll includes the use of baby clothes and a black leather jacket. The wording has been changed somewhat from the original.

Stevenson, Robert Louis. *Block City.* Illustrated by Ashley Wolff. Dutton, 1988.

This picture version of Stevenson's poem shows a young boy drifting off to sleep after building a castle and turrets with his blocks. In his dream the whole scene comes alive with knights, sailors, and kings. This book is a wonderful introduction to the works of Robert Louis Stevenson.

Suyeoka, George. *Momotaro: Peach Boy.* Island Heritage/Raintree, 1972, 1989.

This Japanese folktale is the story of an extraordinary boy who is determined to rid his village of the ogres who have terrorized the inhabitants for a year. Momotaro, born from a peach, journeys to Ogre Island to conquer the demons with the help of his animal friends.
JAPANESE CULTURE

Tresselt, Alvin. *The Mitten.* Lothrop, 1964.

When a child drops a mitten in the cold, snowy woods, it quickly becomes a home in which some forest animals can keep warm. More and more animals try to push their way in until the mitten can stretch no more. Jan Brett recently has adapted and illustrated another delightful version of this humorous Ukrainian folktale.

Wall, Lina Mao. *Judge Rabbit and the Tree Spirit.* Adapted by Cathy Spagnoli. Illustrated by Nancy Hom. Children's Book Press, 1991.

Judge Rabbit is a gentle, self-confident creature who is always called on to help people in need. He is one of the most popular figures in Cambodian storytelling. In this tale Judge Rabbit helps a young couple outwit a mischievous tree spirit. The text is bilingual in English and Khmer.

KHMER • CAMBODIAN CULTURE

Wells, Rosemary. *Peabody*. Dial Books, 1983.

Peabody, the bear, is a special birthday gift to Annie. Her love for him helps him feel real. But Peabody is forgotten when Rita, the talking doll, arrives. Do not miss Wells's other books, including *Hazel's Amazing Mother, Noisy Nora*, and *Shy Charles*.

Westcott, Nadine Bernard. *The Lady with the Alligator Purse*. Little, 1988.

This well-known rhyme tells the tale of the lively little boy who tries to eat the bathtub. The doctor, the nurse, and the lady with the alligator purse are called in to diagnose the small boy's ailment. The illustrations are zany and appealing!

Williams, Vera B. *Cherries and Cherry Pits*. Greenwillow, 1986.

In this charming story, a little girl loves to tell stories about the colorful pictures she draws. Her stories incorporate family and neighborhood characters in imaginative tales of sharing and giving to one another.

Wilson, Sarah. *Uncle Albert's Flying Birthday*. Simon and Schuster, 1991.

Jennifer Justine and her brother, William, must take their baths after all when a sleepy baker puts soap powder instead of flour in Uncle Albert's birthday cake. Any child who has ever refused to take a bath will enjoy this bouncy and bubbly adventure.

Winter, Paula. *The Bear and the Fly*. Crown, 1976, 1987.

As the wordless story begins, three bears are enjoying dinner. Unfortunately, a fly arrives and begins to bother everybody. Father Bear desperately tries to get rid of the fly and return to his once peaceful meal. Chaos ensues in this hilarious tale.

Yolen, Jane. *The Emperor and the Kite*. Illustrated by Ed Young. Putnam, 1967, 1988.

This Chinese folktale tells how the smallest daughter of the Emperor rescues her imprisoned father from a high tower. By cleverly flying a kite with a rope attached as the kite's tail, she outsmarts her father's enemies and brings him to safety.

CHINESE CULTURE

EMOTIONS—FEARS, SADNESS, AND JOY

Breinburg, Petronella. *Shawn Goes to School*. Illustrated by Errol Lloyd. Harper Junior, 1974.

Shawn wants to go to preschool; but the first day is scary, and he cries. Things get better soon, and he begins to enjoy school. The illustrations depict an African-American child.

Carle, Eric. ***The Grouchy Ladybug.*** Harper Junior, 1977.

A grouchy ladybug flies away after an argument with a friendly ladybug. The grouchy ladybug is so upset that he tries to start a fight with every animal he meets. Will the argument ruin his whole day? Carle's other books include *Animals, Animals* (a poetry collection), *The Busy Spider, Do You Want to Be My Friend?* and *The Mixed-Up Chameleon.*

Carlson, Nancy. ***Harriet's Recital.*** Carolrhoda, 1982.

Harriet loves to dance, but once a year her ballet class gives a recital. For a week she worries and frets about the event. When the big day arrives, Harriet still insists she cannot perform. With her teacher's support and encouragement, Harriet overcomes her stage fright and begins dancing.

Clifton, Lucille. ***Everett Anderson's Goodbye.*** Illustrated by Ann Grifalconi. Holt, 1983.

Everett tries to understand why his father has died, but he just cannot. Maybe he should have been a better boy; maybe then it would not have happened. With Everett, the listener struggles through the various stages of grief to reach a point of acceptance and peace.

Cohen, Miriam. ***Will I Have a Friend?*** Illustrated by Lillian Hoban. Macmillan, 1967.

This is the first in a series of three stories about early school experiences and going to kindergarten. Jim feels alone, scared, and anxious until he and Paul become friends. The other books in the series are *Best Friends* and *The New Teacher.*

Crowe, Robert L. ***Tyler Toad and the Thunder.*** Illustrated by Kay Chorao. Dutton, 1980.

Toad fears thunder, and none of the other animals can comfort him with their fanciful tales of its source. When the thunder comes again, all the other animals jump into the same hole with Toad, leaving their bravado behind. The colorful illustrations depict the various explanations in a cheerful way.

Hilleary, Jane Kopper. ***Fletcher and the Great Big Dog.*** Illustrated by Richard Brown. Houghton Mifflin, 1988.

When Fletcher encounters the big red dog while riding his Big Wheel around the block, he decides to make a fast getaway and leave the dog behind. Then Fletcher realizes that he is lost and the sky looks quite stormy. The big red dog helps Fletcher find his way back home.

Hong, Lily Toy. ***How the Ox Star Fell from Heaven.*** Whitman, 1990.

In this Chinese tale, readers learn how the oxen came to be the beast of burden in the fields rather than the well-treated beast of the heavens. The beautiful, stylized illustrations add extra delight to this well-told tale.

CHINESE CULTURE

Jonas, Ann. *Holes and Peeks*. Greenwillow, 1984.

A young child is afraid of holes unless they are fixed, plugged, or made smaller. This reassuring book allows the child to peek through holes that are less frightening, such as a buttonhole.

Kantrowitz, Mildred. *Willy Bear*. Illustrated by Nancy Winslow Parker. Macmillan, 1976.

Getting ready for bed can be a traumatic event for a child. In this story the young boy transfers all of his uneasiness to his bear, Willy. This allows the boy to offer advice and share some worries and fears (e.g., a night-light). Finally, he brings the bear to bed with him so that Willy won't be quite so lonely.

Keller, Holly. *Goodbye, Max*. Greenwillow, 1987.

This is a warm, wise, and reassuring story about loving a pet, losing a pet, and then sharing the grief. The vet does everything possible, but still, Ben's dog, Max, dies. Ben begins to feel better when he and his friend, Zach, begin remembering funny things Max had done, and they can laugh—and cry—and share memories about Max.

Mayer, Mercer. *There's a Nightmare in My Closet*. Dial Books, 1968.

Certain that a nightmare-monster is hiding in his closet, a worried boy decides to face his fears boldly. To his surprise he finds a timid, frightened, but lovable monster who finds comfort sharing the boy's bed. This book is available in Spanish translation as *Hay una Pesadilla en Mi Armario*.

SPANISH

Peet, Bill. *The Kweeks of Kookatumdee*. Houghton Mifflin, 1985.

The birdlike tweeks are starving because their island does not have enough ploppolop fruit trees to feed them all, until Quentin makes an amazing discovery.

Szilagyi, Mary. *Thunderstorm*. Bradbury, 1985.

When an approaching thunderstorm announces its arrival, a young child rushes home to her mother for security and protection. The little girl experiences various emotions until the storm finally passes.

Varley, Susan. *Badger's Parting Gifts*. Lothrop, 1984.

This story offers a sensitive portrayal of the life and death of a very special friend. Badger's animal friends, feeling overwhelmed by their loss, begin to share warm and loving memories of their friend. These memories represent Badger's lasting gifts to them. It is available in Spanish as *Gracias Tejón*.

SPANISH

> "ALLOW TIME FOR CLASS AND HOME DISCUSSIONS AFTER READING A STORY. THOUGHTS, HOPES, FEARS, AND DISCOVERIES ARE AROUSED BY A BOOK."
>
> JIM TRELEASE
> *THE READ-ALOUD HANDBOOK*
> 1984, P. 67

Viorst, Judith. ***The Tenth Good Thing About Barney.*** Illustrated by Eric Blegvad. Macmillan, 1971, 1987, 1988.

When a pet cat named Barney dies, the young owner tries to deal with his loss and find comfort. He identifies many good things about his cat and, in doing so, eases his pain and builds beautiful memories. Suitable for all listeners and readers.

Wilhelm, Hans. ***I'll Always Love You.*** Crown, 1985, 1989.

When a young boy loses his pet dog, Elfie, nothing can replace that loss. When a neighbor offers a new puppy to the boy, he feels that he is not quite ready for a new pet. Instead, he gives Elfie's basket to the neighbor to use. This book is available in Spanish as *Yo Siempre Te Querré.*

SPANISH

II
THE CHILD'S HOME AND FAMILY

FAMILY RELATIONSHIPS

Ackerman, Karen. *Song and Dance Man.* Illustrated by Stephen Gammell. Knopf, 1988.

When Grandpa takes his grandchildren to the attic, good times are in store. He dazzles them with his old vaudeville song-and-dance routines. The attic holds many special memories and reminders of days gone by, but Grandpa prefers the present days with his grandchildren.

Adoff, Arnold. *Black Is Brown Is Tan.* Illustrated by Emily McCully. Harper Junior, 1973.

This story told in poem-song form tells about a family's love for each other and everything around them. The mother is brown-skinned; the father is white-skinned; and the children are a variety of skin colors. The watercolor illustrations blend beautifully with the text.

Albert, Burton. *Where Does the Trail Lead?* Illustrated by Brian Pinkney. Simon and Schuster, 1991.

With the smell of the sea always in his nostrils, a boy follows an island path through flowers and pine needles, over the dunes, to a reunion with his family. The illustrations depict a black family.

Alexander, Martha. *Nobody Asked Me If I Wanted a Baby Sister.* Dial Books, 1971.

Sometimes, baby sisters can get in the way. The young boy in this story decides that he will give his sister away. But then he discovers that she likes him. This humorous story is a surprisingly realistic look at brothers and sisters.

Aliki. *The Two of Them.* Greenwillow (1979); Morrow (1987).

This tender story about family bonding across generations is about a grandfather and his grandchild. The special friendship and love that they share with each other from birth to death is beautifully presented. This story is a gentle, poignant portrayal of the changes that life and death bring to us.

Baum, Louis. *One More Time.* Illustrated by Paddy Bouma. Morrow, 1986.

Simon and Dad spend a Sunday afternoon in the park. At day's end they say good-bye, knowing there will be another time. Rich with gentle humor, this charming portrait of a small boy and his father unfolds in softly drawn pictures that have a warm wash of color.

Blaustein, Muriel. *Play Ball, Zachary!* Harper Junior, 1988.

Zachary the tiger cub and his dad are good at different things. His dad wants him to play sports, and Zachary wants to read and draw but most of all not to disappoint Dad. Bright, cartoonish drawings illustrate the different kinds of ability.

★ Brown, Margaret Wise. *The Runaway Bunny*. Illustrated by Clement Hurd. Harper Junior, 1942, 1972, 1977.

In this fanciful tale, a little bunny threatens to run away from his mother. Young children love finding the bunny in his various hiding places: the garden, the circus, or on the mountain. Other books by Brown include *The Important Book* and *The Little Fur Family*.

Bunting, Eve. *The Wednesday Surprise.* Illustrated by Donald Carrick. Clarion, 1989.

Grandma visits her grandchild every Wednesday. After dinner is over, they sit and read together; but Grandma is unable to read. Anna teaches her so that Grandma can surprise the family by reading a story to Anna's father on his upcoming birthday. The "Wednesday surprise" turns out to be a wonderful present for all!

Butler, Dorothy. *My Brown Bear Barney.* Illustrated by Elizabeth Fuller. Greenwillow, 1989.

The young narrator of this story discusses the various places she visits and the things that she takes with her. Always included on the list is her brown bear, Barney. The book illustrates the concept of relationships at two different levels: interacting with family members and choosing items that go with an activity.

Caines, Jeannette. *I Need a Lunch Box.* Harper Junior, 1988.

While watching his sister prepare for school, a younger brother decides that he needs to have a lunch box, also. He dreams about having a different colored lunch box for each day of school. On his sister's first day of school, he gets a happy surprise. The illustrations depict an African-American family.

Caines, Jeannette. *Just Us Women.* Illustrated by Pat Cummings. Harper Junior, 1982.

This story is about relationships and travel. A young girl and her favorite aunt plan an exciting trip by car together. The bonding that they experience makes the trip and the planning worthwhile. The illustrations portray African-Americans.

Carlson, Natalie Savage. *Runaway Marie Louise.* Illustrated by José Aruego and Ariane Dewey. Scribner, 1977.

Marie Louise, a brown mongoose, runs away after her mother spanks her for being naughty. She goes searching for a new mama.

Clifton, Lucille. *Everett Anderson's Nine Month Long.* Illustrated by Ann Grifalconi. Holt, 1987.

Everett Anderson is waiting for a new brother or sister. He finds it quite difficult to be patient. The story of anticipating a new baby in the family is told in gentle, loving, accurate detail from Everett's point of view. Illustrations depict an African-American family.

Cohen, Barbara. *Molly's Pilgrim.* Illustrated by Michael J. Deraney. Lothrop, 1983.

Molly is a new immigrant to the United States from Russia. At school, children make fun of her differences. For a Thanksgiving project Molly represents *her* culture and her understanding of what being a pilgrim means to many newcomers.

De Paola, Tomie. *Nana Upstairs and Nana Downstairs.* Putnam, 1973.

Tommy visits two grandmothers: one is a bustling, active "downstairs" nana; and the other is a great grandmother who stays upstairs. After Nana upstairs dies, Tommy is comforted by his mother, who tells him that Nana now sends him kisses in the form of shooting stars.

De Paola, Tomie. *Watch Out for the Chicken Feet in Your Soup.* Prentice Hall, 1974.

Joey brings his special friend, Eugene, along on a visit to his "Old World" Grandma. Eugene enjoys his visit and thoroughly appreciates Grandma's fresh, exciting ways. Joey gets another view of Grandma too, and he grows to appreciate her even more. Other popular books by De Paola include *Big Anthony and the Magic Ring, Four Stories and Four Seasons, The Legend of the Bluebonnet, The Legend of the Indian Paintbrush, Marianna May and Nursey,* and *Now One Step, Now the Other.*

Dragonwagon, Crescent. *Home Place.* Illustrated by Jerry Pinkney. Macmillan, 1990.

While out hiking, a family comes on the site of an old house and finds some clues about the people who once lived there. Jerry Pinkney's brilliant, full-color illustrations are rich in feeling and detail and vivid in color and emotional tone.

★ Eastman, P. D. *Are You My Mother?* Random, 1960.

A newly hatched bird finds itself alone in its nest without a mother. To everyone that it meets, it asks the same question, "Are you my mother?" The baby bird is finally rescued by a steam-shovel operator who returns the baby bird to its nest and mother. This book is translated into Spanish as *¿Eres Tú Mi Mamá?*

SPANISH

★ Flack, Marjorie. *Angus and the Cat.* Doubleday, 1931, 1989.

Readers encounter Angus, a curious Scottish terrier, in this series of books dealing with Angus's varied adventures. In this selection a cat is added to the family household. This means adjustment time for all—especially Angus. This book is available in Spanish as *Angus y el Gato.*

SPANISH

Flournoy, Valerie. *The Patchwork Quilt.* Illustrated by Jerry Pinkney. Dial Books, 1985.

A loving is told story about a grandmother who starts a quilt and becomes too ill to complete it. Her granddaughter and other members of the family help to finish it while she recovers. This story shows the bonding and love of an African-American family.

Foreman, Michael. *Ben's Baby.* Harper Junior, 1988.

Children sometimes have unusual requests when birthdays come around. Ben has decided that he wants a baby for his birthday. This tender story describes how he gets his wish.

Fox, Mem. *Koala Lou, I'll Always Love You.* Illustrated by Pamela Lofts. 1988, 1989.

Koala Lou thinks her mother does not love her anymore because there are so many younger koalas in her family. Koala Lou plans to win the Bush Olympics so her mother will once again say, "Koala Lou, I'll always love you!" This is a reassuring story for the child who feels jealous of a new sibling.

★ Freeman, Donald. *Corduroy.* Viking/Puffin, 1968.

Corduroy, a teddy bear, wants to be loved and cared for. As he sits on the shelf of the department store, he keeps hoping that someone will buy him and take him home. Lisa, a little girl, gives him a home and love. *Corduroy* is available in a Spanish translation. More adventures of Corduroy continue in a sequel, *A Pocket for Corduroy.*
SPANISH

Goffstein, M. B. *Brookie and Her Lamb.* Farrar, 1981.

This simple, fanciful tale describes a young girl who loves her lamb so much that she creates storybooks and songbooks with the script, "Bah-bah-bah." In doing this, Brookie is sure that her lamb will be able to read them very well.

Greenfield, Eloise. *She Come Bringing Me That Little Baby Girl.* Illustrated by John Steptoe. Lippincott, 1974.

Kevin finds it difficult to accept a baby sister instead of the baby brother that he had wanted. Later, Kevin realizes that Mother's arms and love are for both him and his sister. Feeling better about his place in the family, Kevin is able to discover the importance of his role as big brother.

Guarino, Deborah. *Is Your Mama a Llama?* Illustrated by Steven Kellogg. Scholastic, 1989.

This book begs to be read aloud as Lloyd, the llama, meets a variety of animals and inquires whether their mamas are llamas. After each animal's mother has been described, the page is turned, and the identity of the animal is revealed.

Hill, Eric. *Where's Spot?* Putnam, 1980.

Young Spot is missing, and his mother cannot find him anywhere. She looks all over the house—under the bed, in the closet, and in other common places in the house. By lifting tabs and flaps on each page, children encounter animals and household items in this vocabulary-building book for toddlers. Other books about Spot include *Spot Goes to School, Spot's Christmas,* and *Spot's First Walk.* Spanish translations are *¿Dónde Está Spot? El Primer Paseo de Spot, La Primer Navidad de Spot,* and *Spot Va a la Escuela.*
SPANISH

Hofstrand, Mary. *By the Sea.* Macmillan, 1989.

A young piglet tells about his adventures with his family when his parents take him to the seashore. He recounts the marvelous things that his family is unable to do at home but manages to do by the sea. The story is told in rhymed verse with old-fashioned illustrations.

Hughes, Shirley. *Dogger* (Also appears as *David and Dog*). Lothrop, 1988.

When David loses his favorite stuffed dog at the school fair, his sister, Bella, comes to his rescue. This story illustrates the cooperation and warmth between siblings in day-to-day interactions and problem solving.

Hutchins, Pat. *The Doorbell Rang.* Greenwillow, 1986.

Mother has made cookies for Victoria and Sam to share—cookies "as good as Grandma's." But the ringing doorbell brings many friends with whom to share the cookies, until there is only one cookie per child. When the doorbell rings again, Grandma arrives with a whole sheet of cookies for the family.

Hutchins, Pat. *Happy Birthday, Sam.* Greenwillow, 1978.

It is Sam's birthday. He is a whole year older but not much bigger. He still cannot reach the light switch or his clothes in the closet or the taps on the sink in the bathroom. But Grandpa sends him a little chair "just the right size" that allows him to solve all those problems.

Johnson, Angela. *Do Like Kyla.* Illustrated by James E. Ransome. Orchard, 1990.

This simple story is about the importance of big sisters and how younger siblings like to mimic all their actions. The reader experiences a day in the life of a young black girl who shows us what it is like to follow the leader.

Johnson, Angela. *Tell Me a Story, Mama.* Illustrated by David Sonam. Orchard, 1989.

A young girl asks her mother to tell her a bedtime story about the mother's childhood. The book encourages an awareness of continuity in a family's history. The mother's active listening evokes memories and wise reflections. The soft watercolor illustrations add to the overall effect of the story.

Johnston, Tony. *The Quilt Story.* Illustrated by Tomie de Paola. Putnam, 1985.

Linking the past with the present is one of the themes that runs through this story. A pioneer mother makes a quilt for her daughter. This heirloom is passed down from generation to generation until a new young girl discovers the quilt in the attic. The quilt becomes an important part of her life and a reminder of her heritage.

★ Keats, Ezra Jack. *Peter's Chair.* Harper Junior, 1967, 1983.

Peter feels left out and resentful when his parents begin painting and preparing for the arrival of a new baby. Peter decides to keep his little chair and run away. When he finally

> "**S**TUDIES HAVE SHOWN THAT READING ALOUD TO CHILDREN SIGNIFICANTLY BROADENS THEIR READING INTERESTS AND TASTES."
>
> MARGARET MARY KIMMEL AND ELIZABETH SEGEL
> *FOR READING OUT LOUD!
> A GUIDE TO SHARING BOOKS
> WITH CHILDREN*
> P. 22

realizes that the chair is too small for him, he helps Dad paint the chair for his new sister. Other books by Keats that feature Peter are *Goggles, A Letter to Amy, The Snowy Day,* and *Whistle for Willie.*

Keller, Holly. ***Goodbye, Max.*** Greenwillow, 1987.

This is a warm, wise, and reassuring story about loving a pet, losing a pet, and then sharing the grief. The vet had done everything possible, but still, Ben's dog, Max, dies. Ben begins to feel better when he and his friend, Zach, begin remembering funny things Max had done, and they can laugh—and cry—and share memories about Max.

Kraus, Robert. ***Another Mouse to Feed.*** Illustrated by José Aruego and Ariane Dewey. Macmillan, 1980.

Mr. and Mrs. Mouse have their hands full with 32 mice children when an orphan mouse is left on their doorstep. When they take him in, the strain that results causes them to collapse. The mouse children come to the rescue by helping out and keeping things running.

Kraus, Robert. ***Leo the Late Bloomer.*** Illustrated by José Aruego. Harper Junior, 1987.

Leo, a young tiger, cannot do anything right. He cannot read or write, and he is very sloppy. His father is concerned, but his mother says, "He's just a late bloomer." Leo's father watches and watches until he forgets to watch any longer. And then one day—Leo blooms! This book is available in a Spanish translation.

SPANISH

Kraus, Robert. ***Whose Mouse Are You?*** Illustrated by José Aruego. Macmillan, 1972.

When Little Mouse decides that no one loves him, he runs away. His parents find him at a phone booth near his home. This book is also available in a Spanish translation, *¿De Quién Eres Ratoncito?* Do not miss the sequel to this book, *Where Are You Going, Little Mouse?*

SPANISH

Levinson, Riki. ***I Go with My Family to Grandma's.*** Illustrated by Diane Goode. Dutton, 1986.

When a reunion is planned at Grandma's house, relatives travel from different parts of the city by different means to arrive for the special occasion. This warm, nurturing book will make children want to share memories of getting together with their friends and relatives.

Lobel, Arnold. ***Mouse Tales.*** Harper Junior, 1972.

Mouse Tales is a collection of seven bedtime stories that Papa Mouse agrees to tell his seven sons as they prepare for a night's sleep. Small illustrations and rebuses complement the simple text and make this book an enjoyable listening experience for preschoolers. The translation available in Spanish is *Historias de Ratones.*

SPANISH

Loh, Morag. *Tucking Mommy In.* Illustrated by Donna Rawlins. Orchard, 1987.

When Mommy comes home from work exhausted and worn out, the children of the family (a young brother and sister) try to make her comfortable. This is a warm and sensitive book about love and caring.

★ Marshall, James. *The Three Little Pigs.* Dial Books, 1989.

The reader encounters a dressed-up version of the old tale about the pig brothers and their wisdom and folly. The cartoonlike illustrations add additional humor to the text. A Spanish version of this story is available.

SPANISH

Martinez i Vendrell, María. *Un Hermano para Celia.* Illustrated by Roser Capdevila. Destino, 1986.

In this hilarious and educational story about sibling jealousy, Celia deals with the feelings of confusion when she experiences the arrival of a new baby brother. This is another title in the series LET'S TALK ABOUT . . . . It is available in English/Chinese and English/Vietnamese from Magi Publications, London.

CHINESE • SPANISH • VIETNAMESE

Miller, Montzalee. *My Grandmother's Cookie Jar.* Illustrated by Katherine Potter. Price Stern, 1987.

When the gifts of a child's cultural heritage are shared, the spirit of Grandma lives on. This is a beautiful story of American Indians.

AMERICAN INDIAN CULTURE

Murphy, Jill. *Five Minutes' Peace.* Putnam, 1986.

All that Mrs. Large, an elephant mother, wants is five minutes' peace from her wonderful, rambunctious children. But when she decides to escape for a five-minute soak in the bathtub, chaos follows. This British import will delight children from any country because of the universal treatment of family interaction and interdependence. Listeners will also enjoy *Peace at Last* by this author.

Parramón, José María, and Carme Sole Vendrell. *Los Padres.* Illustrated by María Rius. Barron, 1987.

Los Padres is one of four books about the family. Others in the series are *Los Abuelos* (grandparents), *Los Jovenes* (teenagers), and *Los Niños* (children). *Los Padres* is about parents.

SPANISH

Polacco, Patricia. *The Keeping Quilt.* Simon and Schuster, 1988.

When Great-Grandma Anna came to America, she learned English in school; however, to remind herself of the old country, she made a quilt. The heritage of the family is recollected through the various uses of the quilt. Four generations are depicted in this story. The keeping quilt becomes a symbol of love and faith.

Rosen, Michael. ***We're Going on a Bear Hunt.*** Illustrated by Helen Oxenbury. Macmillan, 1989.

This new version of an old tale rhythmically follows the family in search of their quarry, the bear. Rosen has added delightful participation sound effects to his version. When the quarry is found, a return trip is in order, with all the difficulties encountered again.

Rylant, Cynthia. ***The Relatives Came.*** Illustrated by Stephen Gammell. Bradbury, 1985.

The author relates the story of a visit by relatives and all the excitement and activities associated with such an event. Poignant, humorous illustrations blend with the story to convey the happy closeness of a boisterous, loving family reunited.

Scott, Ann Herbert. ***On Mother's Lap.*** Illustrated by Glo Coalson. McGraw-Hill, 1972.

A young Eskimo child appreciates the cozy security of rocking in mother's lap. The fear of losing this closeness is evident with the arrival of a new baby. The story depicts the universal bonding that occurs between a mother and child.

★ Segal, Lore. ***Tell Me a Mitzi.*** Illustrated by Harriet Pincus. Farrar, 1970.

When Mitzi, a young girl, asks her parents to tell a story about her, the story becomes a "Mitzi." This book includes three such stories about Mitzi; her younger brother, Jacob; and the family. The vividly detailed, funny illustrations fit the text. Segal has also written *Tell Me a Trudy.*

Simon, Norman. ***All Kinds of Families.*** Illustrated by Joe Lasker. Whitman, 1975.

This concept book about families shows the variety of family compositions and patterns. The loving, supportive, sharing nature of family life is portrayed through a simple, direct text. The story text is illustrated with pen-and-ink drawings.

★ Steig, William. ***Sylvester and the Magic Pebble.*** Simon and Schuster, 1969.

On a rainy day, Sylvester finds a red magic pebble that makes wishes come true. A surprise attack from a lion causes Sylvester to make a wish that he cannot change. When he is finally back home with his parents, he finds that he has everything he needs. A translation is available in Spanish, *Silvestre y la Piedrita Mágica.*

SPANISH

Steptoe, John. **Baby Says.** Lothrop, 1988.

In this repetitive text, the listener finds a delightful story of a big brother figuring out how to include his baby brother in his play. A strong sense of sibling love is conveyed in the story, both through the pictures and the text. The illustrations depict an African-American family.

★ Steptoe, John. **Stevie.** Harper Junior, 1969.

Bobby, a young African-American boy, does not like the problems that having a foster brother creates. Bobby finds it very difficult to adapt to this intruding child. When Stevie has to leave, Bobby finally acknowledges how much he misses his new friend.

Titherington, Jeanne. **A Place for Ben.** Greenwillow, 1987.

When the new baby brother arrives, Ben feels different, especially because Ezra's crib is moved into his room. Ben goes elsewhere in search of a place of his own but soon decides that he is much happier *with* people than *without* them, including his little brother. This is a personal awareness book that deals with sibling rivalry.

Vincent, Gabrielle. **Smile, Ernest and Celestine.** Greenwillow, 1982.

A mischievous little mouse, Celestine, discovers a drawer full of photographs. When Ernest learns that Celestine is disappointed because she does not find any pictures of herself among the collection, Ernest resolves to create a very special photo album that will lift her spirits.

Viorst, Judith. **The Tenth Good Thing About Barney.** Illustrated by Eric Blegvad. Macmillan, 1971, 1987, 1988.

When a pet cat named Barney dies, the young owner tries to deal with his loss and find comfort. He identifies many good things about his cat and, in doing so, eases his pain and builds beautiful memories. This story is suitable for all listeners and readers.

Waber, Bernard. **Funny, Funny Lyle.** Houghton Mifflin, 1987.

Lyle, the crocodile, experiences many changes in his life when his mother moves in with the Primm family and Mrs. Primm announces she is expecting a baby.

Wahl, Jan. **Humphrey's Bear.** Illustrated by William Joyce. Holt, 1987.

After his father says Humphrey is too old for his teddy bear, Humphrey's bear takes him on a magical dreamland boat ride away from the world of adults. When Humphrey awakens, his father and the bear are there to provide comfort and security.

Watanabe, Shigeo. **Daddy, Play with Me!** Illustrated by Yasuo Ohtomo. Putnam, 1986.

Daddy and Baby Bear play horse-and-rider, make a train, and fly a plane until Daddy is exhausted. Then it is nap time for both. This book is part of the I Love to Do Things with Daddy series, which is popular as story-time reading for the very young child.

Wellington, Monica. *Molly Chelsea and Her Calico Cat.* Dutton, 1988.

Molly is ready to go out shopping for fruit, fish, and other treats for herself and her pet cat. While Molly is gone, the cat creates quite a mess before she settles down in Molly's soft shoe for a nap! The bold print and colorful illustrations are appealing to young children.

Wells, Rosemary. *Max's First Word.* Dial Books, 1979.

Young children will enjoy Wells's lovable toddler rabbit, Max, and his extremely talkative sister, Ruby. In this book Max learns to talk. Other books in the series include *Max's New Suit, Max's Ride, Max's Toys: A Counting Book,* and *Say Apple, Max.*

Wells, Rosemary. *Noisy Nora.* Dial Books, 1973, 1980.

When Nora feels left out, she tries to get everybody's attention by being quite noisy. Being noisy does not work, so she decides to hide. When she is found, Nora decides that she does not have to be noisy after all. Other books for the young listener by Wells are *Good Night, Fred; A Lion for Lewis; Shy Charles;* and *Timothy Goes to School.*

" . . . Children who are not told stories and who are not read to will have few reasons for wanting to read."

Gail E. Haley
American Author

Wilhelm, Hans. *I'll Always Love You.* Crown, 1985, 1989.

When a young boy loses his pet dog, Elfie, nothing can replace that loss. When a neighbor offers a new puppy to the boy, he feels that he is not quite ready for a new pet. Instead, he gives Elfie's basket to the neighbor to use. This book is available in Spanish as *Yo Siempre Te Querré.*

SPANISH

Wilhelm, Hans. *Oh, What a Mess!* Crown, 1988.

Franklin prides himself on being neat and clean. He is ashamed to have friends visit his home, because his family is lazy and the house is an absolute mess. When Franklin wins the art contest at the school, there is no clean place to display his painting until the family springs into action. This book helps children explore personal pride and family bonding. Another popular book by this author is *Let's Be Friends Again!*

Williams, Barbara. *Kevin's Grandma.* Illustrated by Kay Chorao. Dutton, 1975.

Kevin has a most unusual grandmother. She does not like to stay home and play checkers and make popcorn balls as other, "traditional" grandmothers do. Kevin's grandmother rides a Honda 90 motorcycle, shingles the roof, takes judo lessons, and belongs to a mountain-climbing club.

Williams, Vera B. *A Chair for My Mother.* Greenwillow, 1982, 1984.

After a fire destroys the furniture in their apartment, a young girl, her grandmother, and her mother begin saving coins in a jar to replace the mother's comfortable chair. Other current books by Williams include *Music, Music for Everyone;* and *Something Special for Me.*

Williams, Vera. *"More, More, More," said the Baby.* Greenwillow, 1990.

Three brief tales of loving, playful interactions between three toddlers and caring adults are portrayed in rhythmic text and bright, exuberant paintings. The characters are racially diverse.

Yolen, Jane. *No Bath Tonight.* Illustrated by Nancy Winslow Parker. Harper Junior, 1978.

Young Jeremy manages all week to avoid his bath time by telling his mother about all the injuries he has acquired in his adventures. But on Sunday, Grandmother arrives. Grandmother, in her wise and ingenious way, manages to get Jeremy to do what he has avoided all week—take a long-postponed bath.

Yolen, Jane. *Owl Moon.* Illustrated by John Schoenherr. Putnam, 1987.

A child and his father go owling at night on a cold, snowy evening. The listener shares the gorgeous moonlit vistas and the descriptions of what is seen and heard on the excursion. The relationship between father and child shows a bond of love and caring.

Yolen, Jane. *The Three Bears Rhyme Book.* Illustrated by Jane Dyer. Harcourt Brace Jovanovich, 1987.

This collection of rhymes and pictures celebrates the everyday life of Goldilocks and the Three Bears. Events in the book are seen through the eyes of Baby Bear. Goldilocks is presented in a positive way. Other books for young listeners by Yolen include *The Girl Who Loved the Wind, The Lullaby Songbook,* and the COMMANDER TOAD series for early readers.

Zemach, Harve. *Mommy, Buy Me a China Doll.* Illustrated by Margot Zemach. Farrar, 1975.

This rhyming adaptation of an old Ozark mountain children's song can either be spoken or sung. The topic of the rhyme is a child's perennial request for a toy and the bargaining with a parent that sometimes occurs. The illustrations detail the humorous topsy-turviness that would result.

Ziefert, Harriet. *A New Coat for Anna.* Illustrated by Anita Lobel. Knopf, 1986.

During wartime when money was scarce, there was hardly enough food, and finding warm coats was almost impos-

"A CHILD CANNOT HELP BUT BEGIN LIFE WITH A LOVE OF POETRY IF YOU CONSIDER THAT THE FIRST SOUND HE HEARS IS A POEM: THE RHYTHMIC BEAT OF HIS MOTHER'S HEART."

JIM TRELEASE
THE READ-ALOUD HANDBOOK
1984, P. 61

sible. In this story young Anna gets a much-needed new coat because of her mother's resourcefulness and unselfishness. This story is based on actual facts.

Zolotow, Charlotte. *My Grandson, Lew*. Illustrated by William Pene Du Bois. Harper Junior, 1974.

When a child recalls his deceased grandfather late at night, a loving mother comforts him. As they share their unique memories of Grandpa, they find comfort in knowing that they can both miss Grandpa together.

Zolotow, Charlotte. *William's Doll*. Illustrated by William Pene Du Bois. Harper Junior, 1972.

Young William wants a doll more than anything. But everyone, except his grandmother, thinks that having a doll will make William a sissy or a creep. In her wisdom she buys William a doll so that he can learn the responsibility of caring for it and gain practice in being a father. Other titles by Zolotow include *I Like to Be Little, If It Weren't for You, My Friend John, The Quarreling Book,* and *The Storm Book.*

Daily Experiences

Allen, Jeffrey. *Mary Alice, Operator Number 9*. Illustrated by James Marshall. Little, 1975.

When Mary Alice, the town's expert telephone operator duck, becomes ill, disaster strikes. Mary Alice's boss looks for a replacement, but no other animal can fill her position. The boss humorously learns that Mary Alice is irreplaceable. The sequel to this book is *Mary Alice Returns.*

Anderson, Peggy Perry. *Time for Bed, the Baby-sitter Said*. Houghton Mifflin, 1987.

The baby-sitter is trying to put Joe to bed, but Joe will not go. This hilarious tale of a battle of wills is told in rhyme. This should not be missed for children who are past the separation anxiety stage.

Arnold, Tedd. *No Jumping on the Bed!* Dial Books, 1987.

Even though he has been warned many times by his father, a young boy continues to jump on his bed. Finally, the bed crashes through several floors and keeps going down toward the basement of his apartment building.

Bang, Molly. *Ten, Nine, Eight*. Penguin, 1985.

This bedtime counting book reflects the evening activities of a small child and her father as they prepare for bed. The illustrations of this African-American family depict a peaceful and soothing atmosphere, which makes this book perfect for bedtime sharing with a toddler.

★ Brown, Margaret Wise. *Goodnight Moon*. Illustrated by Clement Hurd. Harper Junior, 1947, 1977.

A young rabbit bids "goodnight" to the familiar objects that can be found in his bedroom. The simple rhymes and illustrations capture a sense of cozy comfort. This book is also available in Spanish as *Buenas Noches Luna*.
SPANISH

Brown, Tricia. *Hello, Amigos!* Photographs by Fran Ortiz. Holt, 1986.

Frankie Valdez is a Mexican-American boy who lives in the Mission district of San Francisco. This book tells about a special celebration in his life—his birthday—and the ways that family and friends make the day extra special for Frankie.
MEXICAN-AMERICAN CULTURE

Browne, Anthony. *Things I Like*. Knopf, 1989.

In this simple tale with its uncluttered text, a small chimpanzee enjoys activities such as hiding, acrobatics, building sand castles, and being with friends. Delightful illustrations depict the obvious pleasure of the young chimp as he experiences the world around him. Other books by Browne include *Gorilla, Willy the Champ*, and *Willy the Wimp*.

Cazet, Denys. *Mother Night*. Orchard, 1989.

The baby animals go to sleep as Mother Night hushes the earth, and then they wake up to a new day. The humorous illustrations are soothing and beautiful.

Cazet, Denys. *Never Spit on Your Shoes*. Orchard, 1990.

Arnie, the pup, tells his mother all about his first day of school in the first grade. Arnie's version of the day does not quite match the wonderfully comic events demonstrated by Cazet's whimsical animal characters.

Craft, Ruth. *The Day of the Rainbow*. Illustrated by Niki Daly. Penguin, 1989.

Rhythmic verse and shimmering watercolors tell the story of three troubled people on a hot summer day in the city and the rainbow that brings them together.

Greenfield, Eloise. *Honey, I Love And Other Love Poems*. Illustrated by Leo and Diane Dillon. Harper Junior, 1978.

This collection of short poems captures the ordinary experiences, activities, and emotions of childhood. The illustrations of black children add visual interest and depth to the text.

Hayes, Sarah. *Eat Up, Gemma!* Illustrated by Jan Ormerod. Lothrop, 1988.

Baby Gemma is not interested in eating food. She throws it, squashes it, and gives it to the dog until her brother discovers a clever way to entice her to take a bite. The story depicts the life and community of a black family.

Highwater, Jamake. *Moonsong Lullaby.* Photographs by Marcia Keegan. Lothrop, 1981.

Beautiful photographs highlight this soothing bedtime story of American Indian life.

AMERICAN INDIAN CULTURE

Hines, Anna Grossnickle. *Don't Worry, I'll Find You.* Dutton, 1986.

Mama decides to go shopping at the mall with young Sarah. Sarah wants her doll to go along, but Mother warns that the doll might get lost. When Sarah becomes lost, she stays put and waits for Mother to find her. Other books by Hines include *Come to the Meadow, Maybe a Band-Aid Will Help,* and *Taste the Raindrops.*

Horenstein, Henry. *Sam Goes Trucking.* Houghton Mifflin, 1989.

By means of full-color photographs, the author shows us how Sam spends the day with his trucker father in a sixteen-wheeler.

Isadora, Rachel. *City Seen from A to Z.* Greenwillow, 1983.

Scenes of city life are illustrated in this black-and-white alphabet book. From skyscrapers to subways, adults and children participate in the activities of the city scene. The city's diverse social, economic, cultural, and multiethnic aspects of life are well represented.

Kraus, Robert. *Leo the Late Bloomer.* Illustrated by José Aruego. Harper Junior, 1987.

Leo, a young tiger, cannot do anything right. He cannot read or write, and he is very sloppy. His father is concerned, but his mother says, "He's just a late bloomer." Leo's father watches and watches until he forgets to watch any longer. And then one day—Leo blooms! This book is available in a Spanish translation.

SPANISH

Lindgren, Astrid. *The Tomten.* Illustrated by Harold Wiberg. Putnam, 1961, 1979.

The magical Tomten, a reassuring little gnome, makes his nightly rounds to all the farm creatures, tucking them in on a winter's night.

Lobel, Arnold. *Mouse Tales.* Harper Junior, 1972.

Mouse Tales is a collection of seven bedtime stories that Papa Mouse agrees to tell his seven sons as they prepare for a night's sleep. Small illustrations and rebuses complement the simple text and make this book an enjoyable listening experience for preschoolers. The translation available in Spanish is *Historias de Ratones.*

SPANISH

McPhail, David. *Fix-It.* Dutton, 1984.

Little Emma, a bear, upset because the television set is broken, wakes her parents and demands that they fix the set. While waiting for the repairperson, Emma's parents try various ideas to entertain her, including reading a book to her. Most of the story's humor is conveyed through the illustrations.

Mayer, Mercer. *There's a Nightmare in My Closet.* Dial Books, 1968.

Certain that a nightmare-monster is hiding in his closet, a worried boy decides to face his fears boldly. To his surprise he finds a timid, frightened, but lovable monster who finds comfort sharing the boy's bed. This book is available in Spanish translation as *Hay una Pesadilla en Mi Armario.*

SPANISH

Murphy, Jill. *Five Minutes' Peace.* Putnam, 1986.

All that Mrs. Large, an elephant mother, wants is five minutes' peace from her wonderful, rambunctious children. But when she decides to escape for a five-minute soak in the bathtub, chaos follows. This British import will delight children from any country because of the universal treatment of family interaction and interdependence. Listeners will also enjoy *Peace at Last* by this author.

Oxenbury, Helen. *The Checkup.* Dutton, 1983.

This book is one of many board books and picture books by this author. *The Checkup* is a simple story about a young child's visit to the doctor. Oxenbury's talent of revealing the humorous side of everyday life through simple text and funny illustrations is evident in this selection.

Oxenbury, Helen. *Tom and Pippo Go for a Walk.* Macmillan, 1988.

This simple story of taking a walk with a parent illustrates a nurturing relationship between a little boy and his mother. The boy mirrors the security of this relationship with his toy monkey.

Pryor, Bonnie. *Greenbrook Farm.* Illustrated by Mark Graham. Simon and Schuster, 1991.

Spring at Greenbrook Farm bursts with the new life of many baby animals, including a calf, a filly, chicks, and ducklings, and a new baby in the family.

Rockwell, Anne. *Bear Child's Book of Special Days.* Dutton, 1989.

The months of the year are featured in Rockwell's informative book about annual special events and holidays. The simple text describes a major activity associated with each month. This book shows the sequence of the calendar and builds the concept of time (e.g., days, weeks, months, and years).

Russo, Marisabina. *The Line Up Book.* Greenwillow, 1986.

Sam loves to have everything in a line. He lines up books, cars, and boots. He lines up things from his bedroom all the way to his mother, who is working in the kitchen.

★ Segal, Lore. *Tell Me a Mitzi.* Illustrated by Harriet Pincus. Farrar, 1970.

When Mitzi, a young girl, asks her parents to tell a story about her, the story becomes a "Mitzi." This book includes three such stories about Mitzi; her younger brother, Jacob; and the family. The vividly detailed, funny illustrations fit the text. Segal has also written *Tell Me a Trudy.*

Tsutsui, Yoriko. *Before the Picnic.* Illustrated by Akiko Hayashi. Putnam, 1987.

Sashi is very excited about the family picnic and wants to help get things ready for the special event. Somehow her efforts are not working out the way she planned. But finally, everyone, including Sashi, is ready to go to the park. Other titles by Tsutsui include *Anna in Charge* and *Anna's Secret Friend.*

★ Viorst, Judith. *Alexander and the Terrible, Horrible, No Good, Very Bad Day.* Illustrated by Ray Cruz. Macmillan, 1972, 1987.

Young Alexander is having a terrible day. What can be done about a day this bad? Alexander decides it would be best to move to Australia! For the young reader or listener, it is comforting to know that other people have bad days too! Other books about Alexander and his family include *Alexander, Who Used to Be Rich Last Sunday;* and *I'll Fix Anthony.*

Watson, Clyde. *Catch Me and Kiss Me and Say It Again.* Putnam, 1978, 1983.

This collection of modern Mother Goose rhymes uses a different approach from the more traditional versions. The book follows the daily activities of young children from getting up in the morning to preparing to go to bed.

Weiss, Nicki. *Where Does the Brown Bear Go?* Illustrated by Monica Weiss. Greenwillow, 1989.

In this enchanting bedtime poem, all the animals of the world are on their way home, ready to go to bed. The rhythmic pattern of the story-poem is appealing to children.

Wood, Audrey. *King Bidgood's in the Bathtub.* Illustrated by Don Wood. Harcourt Brace Jovanovich, 1985.

This sumptuously illustrated, humorous tale is about a king who refuses to leave his bathtub. People from his royal court try everything to get him out, but one small page boy finds a solution to the problem.

Yolen, Jane. *No Bath Tonight.* Illustrated by Nancy Winslow Parker. Harper Junior, 1978.

Young Jeremy manages all week to avoid his bath time by telling his mother about all the injuries he has acquired in his adventures. But on Sunday, Grandmother arrives. Grandmother, in her wise and ingenious way, manages to get Jeremy to do what he has avoided all week—take a long-postponed bath.

Yolen, Jane. *The Three Bears Rhyme Book.* Illustrated by Jane Dyer. Harcourt Brace Jovanovich, 1987.

This collection of rhymes and pictures celebrates the everyday life of Goldilocks and the Three Bears. Events in the book are seen through the eyes of Baby Bear. Goldilocks is presented in a positive way. Other books for young listeners by Yolen include *The Girl Who Loved the Wind, The Lullaby Songbook,* and the COMMANDER TOAD series for early readers.

Zemach, Harve. ***Mommy, Buy Me a China Doll.*** Illustrated by Margot Zemach. Farrar, 1975.

This rhyming adaptation of an old Ozark mountain children's song can either be spoken or sung. The topic of the rhyme is a child's perennial request for a toy and the bargaining with a parent that sometimes occurs. The illustrations detail the humorous topsy-turviness that would result.

Zemach, Margot. ***Hush, Little Baby.*** Dutton, 1987.

This lullaby has soothed and amused small children for many years. Zemach's interpretation of the familiar song is highlighted by her charming, humorous illustrations.

FOOD

★ Carle, Eric. ***The Very Hungry Caterpillar.*** Putnam, 1969, 1987.

A very hungry caterpillar eats its way through the pages of this book on its way to becoming a butterfly. The story playfully reinforces the days of the week, different foods, and the life cycle of a caterpillar. This book appears in a Spanish translation as *La Oruga Muy Hambrienta* (1988).
SPANISH

★ De Paola, Tomie. ***Strega Nona.*** Prentice Hall, 1975.

When Strega Nona leaves her helper, Big Anthony, alone with her magic pot of pasta, trouble is sure to happen. Big Anthony is determined to show the village people how the pot works. However, he fails to learn one very important detail—how to stop the pot from making more pasta when there is already enough.

Dragonwagon, Crescent. ***This Is the Bread I Baked for Ned.*** Illustrated by Isadore Seltzer. Macmillan, 1989.

A fellow named Ned gets a nice surprise in this rhythmic story that takes its cue from the expanding lines of "This Is the House That Jack Built": "This is the bread I baked for Ned/ baked for Ned in the morning." An ordinary event is made special by the harmonious union of text and art.

Ehlert, Lois. ***Eating the Alphabet.*** Harcourt Brace Jovanovich, 1989.

In a demonstration of fruits and vegetables from *A* to *Z* with Lois Ehlert's colorful watercolor illustrations, the opening page states: "Apple to Zucchini, come take a look. Start eating your way through this alphabet book."

★ Galdone, Paul. *The Gingerbread Boy.* Clarion, 1975.

This classic cumulative tale is about the gingerbread cookie that comes to life and runs away through the countryside encountering animals and people. Gingerbread Boy announces to all that they can't catch him. But then he meets a clever fox. This title is available in Spanish as *El Hombrecito de Pan Jengibre.*

SPANISH

★ Hoban, Russell. *Bread and Jam for Frances.* Illustrated by Lillian Hoban. Harper Junior, 1964.

Mother Badger decides to let Frances, a fussy eater, eat only what she likes—bread and jam. By suppertime, Frances is singing quietly, "What I am—is tired of jam." Other Frances stories for young listeners are *A Baby Sister for Frances, Bedtime for Frances, A Birthday for Frances,* and *Best Friends for Frances.*

Hong, Lily Toy. *How the Ox Star Fell from Heaven.* Whitman, 1990.

In this Chinese tale, readers learn how the oxen came to be the beast of burden in the fields rather than the well-treated beast of the heavens. The beautiful, stylized illustrations add an extra delight to this well-told tale.

CHINESE CULTURE

★ McCloskey, Robert. *Blueberries for Sal.* Viking, 1948.

Sal and her mother go on an excursion to pick blueberries. Sal wanders off and encounters a bear cub. Soon mother and daughter and mother bear and cub cross paths. This is an old story that can be enjoyed by today's readers and listeners.

Morris, Ann. *Bread, Bread, Bread.* Photographs by Ken Heyman. Lothrop, 1989.

Beautiful photographs capture the commonalities and differences of bread making and bread uses by various cultures around the world. The young listener can observe that the many sizes, shapes, textures, and colors of bread are as varied as the people who eat it.

Mosel, Arlene. *The Funny Little Woman.* Illustrated by Blair Lent. Dutton, 1972.

In this Japanese tale, a funny little woman who loves to laugh chases her runaway dumpling down a hole. She finds herself on an unusual road and must outwit the three-eyed oni in order to return to her home. Variations to this story can be found in *The Teeny-Tiny Woman* by Tomie de Paola, Paul Galdone, and Jane O'Conner.

JAPANESE CULTURE

Peet, Bill. *The Kweeks of Kookatumdee.* Houghton Mifflin, 1985.

The birdlike tweeks are starving because their island does not have enough ploppolop fruit trees to feed them all, until Quentin makes an amazing discovery.

★ Sawyer, Ruth. *Journey Cake, Ho!* Illustrated by Robert McCloskey. Penguin, 1953, 1978.

When times are hard, a young boy sets out down the mountain to find a new life, but his Journey Cake leads him a merry chase. The boy returns home followed by a farmyard full of animals.

Shelby, Anne. *Potluck.* Illustrated by Irene Trivas. Orchard, 1991.

At a potluck everyone brings some favorite thing to eat. Alpha and Betty and all their friends (Acton to Zelda) bring appropriate alphabetical food (asparagus soup to zucchini casserole). The illustrations depict children from many ethnic groups.

Turnip: An Old Russian Folktale. Illustrated by Pierr Morgan. Putnam, 1990.

The turnip seed that Dedoushka planted in the spring grows to such an enormous size that he is unable to pull it out of the ground. He gets the help of his entire family: his wife, his daughter, his dog, his cat, and even a field mouse. Young readers will love the repetition of this cumulative folktale.

CLOTHING

Daly, Niki. *Not So Fast, Songololo.* Macmillan, 1986.

Malusi, whose nickname is Songololo, helps his grandmother, Gogo, travel to the city to go shopping. His hand-me-down tackies (shoes) have holes, and he wishes for some new bright red ones. Vibrant watercolors highlight this South African tale of a boy who likes to do things slowly, in his own way.

AFRICAN CULTURE

De Paola, Tomie. *Charlie Needs a Cloak.* Prentice Hall, 1972, 1982.

To replace his ragged cloak, Charlie, a shepherd boy, must shear his sheep, spin the wool, dye it, weave it, cut it, and sew it. At each step of the way, Charlie has to deal with stubborn sheep who want to keep him from his task. Other books on this theme include *Anna's New Coat* and *Pelle's New Suit.*

Keats, Ezra Jack. *Jennie's Hat.* Harper Junior, 1966, 1985.

When spring arrives, Jennie needs a new hat to wear. The hat she receives is a gorgeous creation, a gift from her feathered friends. Jennie wears her hat proudly. The collage illustrations in this book add visual interest.

Miller, Margaret. *Whose Hat?* Greenwillow, 1988.

In this book the reader is introduced to color photographs of hats and more hats. With each hat, the question is asked, "Whose hat?" Children have the opportunity to guess the occupation of the wearer. Each occupation is illustrated with a grown-up version of the wearer followed by a youthful depiction of children playing the wearer's role.

Moore, Inga. *Fifty Red Night-Caps.* Chronicle, 1988.

When the caps that Nico is carrying to market are stolen by some mischievous monkeys as he is napping, Nico must find a way to get them back. Quite accidentally he solves the problem. A companion story to share with this selection is the wonderful classic *Caps for Sale,* written and illustrated by Esphyr Slobodkina.

Morris, Ann. *Hats, Hats, Hats.* Photographs by Ken Heyman. Lothrop, 1989.

Selected photographs of hats give the young listener a multicultural tour around the world. The listener can observe people from many different cultures who use their hats for many different purposes. This author and illustrator also have a multicultural book entitled *Bread, Bread, Bread.*

Peek, Merle. *Mary Wore Her Red Dress, and Henry Wore His Green Sneakers.* Clarion, 1985, 1988.

Each of Katy Bear's animal friends wears a different color of clothing to her birthday party. The illustrations are colorful.

Rice, Eve. *Oh, Lewis!* Macmillan, 1987.

Lewis is constantly becoming unzipped, untied, and unbuttoned. His mother says, "Oh, Lewis! I wish you would stay done up!" Lewis finally does, but later he cannot figure out how to get "undone." Other enjoyable books by this author include *Benny Bakes a Cake, New Blue Shoes, Sam Who Never Forgets,* and *What Sadie Sang.*

Rogers, Jean. *Runaway Mittens.* Illustrated by Rie Munoz. Greenwillow, 1988.

Pica, a young Eskimo boy, has trouble keeping track of the mittens that his grandmother knit for him. After a snowstorm, Pica again looks for his mittens. He finds them in the box where Pin, the sled dog, had her puppies the night before. Pica admits that now his mittens may have a permanent new home.

ESKIMO CULTURE

Winthrop, Elizabeth. *Shoes.* Illustrated by William Joyce. Harper Junior, 1986.

All types of shoes are described in this book told in rhymed verse. The illustrations add extra meaning and humor to the verse. As the book says, we have "shoes with ribbons, shoes with bows, shoes to skate in when it snows."

Ziefert, Harriet. *A New Coat for Anna.* Illustrated by Anita Lobel. Knopf, 1986.

During wartime when money was scarce, there was hardly enough food, and finding warm coats was almost impossible. In this story young Anna gets a much-needed new coat because of her mother's resourcefulness and unselfishness. This story is based on actual facts.

HOME AND SHELTER

Dragonwagon, Crescent. *Home Place.* Illustrated by Jerry Pinkney. Macmillan, 1990.
While out hiking, a family comes on the site of an old house and finds some clues about the people who once lived there. Jerry Pinkney's brilliant, full-color illustrations are rich in feeling and detail and vivid in color and emotional tone.

Hill, Eric. *Where's Spot?* Putnam, 1980.
Young Spot is missing, and his mother cannot find him anywhere. She looks all over the house—under the bed, in the closet, and in other common places in the house. By lifting tabs and flaps on each page, children encounter animals and household items in this vocabulary-building book for toddlers. Other books about Spot include *Spot Goes to School, Spot's Christmas,* and *Spot's First Walk.* Spanish translations are *¿Dónde Está Spot? El Primer Paseo de Spot, La Primer Navidad de Spot,* and *Spot Va a la Escuela.*
SPANISH

Hoberman, Mary Ann. *A House Is a House for Me.* Illustrated by Betty Fraser. Viking, 1978.
Full of colorful illustrations, this rhyming concept book describes the different kinds of houses in our world. The book is an excellent vocabulary builder and lends itself to active participation by the listeners.

Isadora, Rachel. *City Seen from A to Z.* Greenwillow, 1983.
Scenes of city life are illustrated in this black-and-white alphabet book. From skyscrapers to subways, adults and children participate in the activities of the city scene. The city's diverse social, economic, cultural, and multiethnic aspects of life are well represented.

Krauss, Ruth, and Maurice Sendak. *A Very Special House.* Harper Junior, 1953.
This delightfully silly book for young listeners describes a young boy's ideal but imaginary house. The rhyming text matches the whimsical line drawings. Other books by this author include *The Growing Story* and *Is This Me?*

★ Marshall, James. *The Three Little Pigs.* Dial Books, 1989.
The reader encounters a dressed-up version of the old tale about the pig brothers and their wisdom and folly. The cartoonlike illustrations add additional humor to the text. A Spanish version of this story is available.
SPANISH

Pryor, Bonnie. *The House on Maple Street.* Illustrated by Beth Peck. Morrow, 1987.
Two girls find a tiny cup made of china and an arrowhead in the garden of their new home and wonder who the original owners of these objects may have been. Children will be

curious about their own neighborhood's history and what it may have been like long, long ago.

Ryder, Joanne. *Under the Moon.* Illustrated by Cheryl Harness. Random, 1989.

Mama Mouse teaches her little mouse how to tell where home is by reminding her of its special smells, sounds, and textures. The book contains detailed drawings of animals, plants, and vistas.

Shannon, George. *Lizard's Song.* Illustrated by José Aruego and Ariane Dewey. Greenwillow, 1981.

When Bear wants something, he takes it, but what Bear really wants is Lizard's song. Lizard is happy to share it, but somehow Bear cannot get the song correct. Bear finally learns to sing his own song in his own way.

Wilhelm, Hans. *Oh, What a Mess!* Crown, 1988.

Franklin prides himself on being neat and clean. He is ashamed to have friends visit his home, because his family is lazy and the house is an absolute mess. When Franklin wins the art contest at the school, there is no clean place to display his painting until the family springs into action. This book helps children explore personal pride and family bonding. Another popular book by this author is *Let's Be Friends Again!*

Wood, Audrey. *The Napping House.* Illustrated by Don Wood. Harcourt Brace Jovanovich, 1984.

In this cumulative tale, everyone is peaceful and sleeping until a wakeful flea on a slumbering mouse starts quite a commotion. The rhyme and rhythm of the tale will capture children's attention and make them want to hear the story over and over again. A sound recording is available.

Zemach, Margot. *It Could Always Be Worse: A Yiddish Folktale.* Farrar, 1976.

A poor man complains that his one-room hut is too noisy and crowded for his family of six children. On advice from his religious leader, he brings all the livestock into the house. He learns his lesson when the animals are returned to the barnyard.

FAMILY TRADITIONS AND CULTURAL HERITAGE

Adler, David A. *A Picture Book of George Washington.* Illustrated by John and Alexandra Wallner. Holiday, 1989.

This is one of a series of picture books by Adler. Important events from famous Americans' lives are detailed in the stories. Other biographies by Adler include *A Picture Book of*

Abraham Lincoln; A Picture Book of Benjamin Franklin; A Picture Book of Martin Luther King, Jr.; and *A Picture Book of Thomas Jefferson.*

Aliki. ***The Two of Them.*** Greenwillow (1979); Morrow (1987).

This tender story about family bonding across generations is about a grandfather and his grandchild. The special friendship and love that they share with each other from birth to death is beautifully presented. This story is a gentle, poignant portrayal of the changes that life and death bring to us.

Blood, Charles L., and Martin Link. ***The Goat in the Rug.*** Illustrated by Nancy Winslow Parker. Macmillan, 1976.

The authors humorously describe a Navaho woman using her goat's hair to weave a rug. It is a real story about a real weaver and a real goat.

AMERICAN INDIAN CULTURE

"HAVE AVAILABLE A VARIETY OF BOOKS THAT SHOW THE DIVERSITY WITHIN AND ACROSS HUMAN CULTURES.... CHILDREN NEED TO BE HELPED TO DEVELOP A WORLD VIEW."

TEACHING MULTICULTURAL LITERATURE IN GRADES K—8 1992, P. 49

Cohen, Barbara. ***Molly's Pilgrim.*** Illustrated by Michael J. Deraney. Lothrop, 1983.

Molly is a new immigrant to the United States from Russia. At school, children make fun of her differences. For a Thanksgiving project Molly represents *her* culture and her understanding of what being a pilgrim means to many newcomers.

De Paola, Tomie. ***Watch Out for the Chicken Feet in Your Soup.*** Prentice Hall, 1974.

Joey brings his special friend, Eugene, along on a visit to his "Old World" Grandma. Eugene enjoys his visit and thoroughly appreciates Grandma's fresh, exciting ways. Joey gets another view of Grandma too, and he grows to appreciate her even more. Other popular books by De Paola include *Big Anthony and the Magic Ring, Four Stories and Four Seasons, The Legend of the Bluebonnet, The Legend of the Indian Paintbrush, Marianna May and Nursey,* and *Now One Step, Now the Other.*

Flournoy, Valerie. ***The Patchwork Quilt.*** Illustrated by Jerry Pinkney. Dial Books, 1985.

A loving story is told about a grandmother who starts a quilt and becomes too ill to complete it. Her granddaughter and other members of the family help to finish it while she recovers. This story shows the bonding and love of an African-American family.

Gibbons, Gail. ***Thanksgiving Day.*** Holiday, 1983.

This book presents factual information about the first Thanksgiving and the importance of this holiday for most Americans. The friendship of the Pilgrims and the Indians is discussed as well as the current customs and practices of this holiday. This book is one in a series on traditional American holidays.

Greenfield, Eloise. *Africa Dream*. Illustrated by Carole Byard. Harper Junior, 1989.

Ancestral history of the African-American experience is poetically portrayed in this elegant book. The illustrations help the listener or reader imagine the past. A companion book for sharing might be Greenfield's *Honey, I Love*.

AFRICAN-AMERICAN CULTURE

Johnston, Tony. *The Quilt Story*. Illustrated by Tomie de Paola. Putnam, 1985.

Linking the past with the present is one of the themes that runs through this story. A pioneer mother makes a quilt for her daughter. This heirloom is passed down from generation to generation until a new young girl discovers the quilt in the attic. The quilt becomes an important part of her life and a reminder of her heritage.

Levinson, Riki. *Our Home Is the Sea*. Illustrated by Dennis Luzak. Dutton, 1988.

Life in Hong Kong is portrayed in this beautifully illustrated story of a young boy finishing his last day of school before a vacation. He reflects on how his father and grandfather have made their living from the sea and how he, too, would like to be a fisher.

CHINESE CULTURE

Levinson, Riki. *Watch the Stars Come Out*. Illustrated by Diane Goode. Dutton, 1985.

This story re-creates the journey of two children who are immigrants from the Old World to America at the turn of the century. Their experiences on the voyage and their reactions to New York City are vividly captured in Diane Goode's beautiful illustrations. This book is available in Spanish as *Mira Cómo Salen las Estrellas*.

SPANISH

Lomas Garza, Carmen. *Family Pictures*. Children's Book Press, 1990.

The author describes, in bilingual text, her experiences growing up in a Hispanic community in Texas. This illustrated book is also available in Spanish as *Cuadros de Familia*.

SPANISH

McDermott, Gerald. *Anansi the Spider: A Tale from the Ashanti*. Holt, 1972.

Anansi is a mischief-making spider who falls into many troubles and needs the help of his six children to save him. While trying to reward his sons for their help, Anansi helps put the moon into the sky for all to enjoy. The book is a Caldecott Honor Book depicting the trickster tale from the Ashanti tribe from Ghana.

AFRICAN CULTURE

Miller, Montzalee. *My Grandmother's Cookie Jar*. Illustrated by Katherine Potter. Price Stern, 1987.

When the gifts of a child's cultural heritage are shared, the spirit of Grandma lives on. This is a beautiful story of American Indians.

AMERICAN INDIAN CULTURE

Morris, Ann. *Loving.* Photographs by Ken Heyman. Lothrop, 1990.

This book of photographs shows families from all over the world helping, talking, playing, sharing, and loving. Family bonding is a universal theme even though foods, clothing, customs, and traditions may differ from region to region. The index gives additional background on the 28 photographs used in the book.

Polacco, Patricia. *The Keeping Quilt.* Simon and Schuster, 1988.

When Great-Grandma Anna came to America, she learned English in school; however, to remind herself of the old country, she made a quilt. The heritage of the family is recollected through the various uses of the quilt. Four generations are depicted in this story. The keeping quilt becomes a symbol of love and faith.

Pryor, Bonnie. *The House on Maple Street.* Illustrated by Beth Peck. Morrow, 1987.

Two girls find a tiny cup made of china and an arrowhead in the garden of their new home and wonder who the original owners of these objects may have been. Children will be curious about their own neighborhood's history and what it may have been like long, long ago.

Rockwell, Anne. *Bear Child's Book of Special Days.* Dutton, 1989.

The months of the year are featured in Rockwell's informative book about annual special events and holidays. The simple text describes a major activity associated with each month. This book shows the sequence of the calendar and builds the concept of time (e.g., days, weeks, months, and years).

Rylant, Cynthia. *When I Was Young in the Mountains.* Illustrated by Diane Goode. Dutton, 1982.

On each page of this book, the author recalls some aspect of life when she was "young in the mountains." The reader experiences the activities and the personalities as well as the customs and the traditions that were a part of growing up in the mountains.

Smucker, Anna Egan. *No Star Nights.* Illustrated by Steve Johnson. Knopf, 1989.

Life in a steel mill town during the 1930s is recalled in this reflective story about family times, games with friends, and going to school when the mill was the dominating focus of everyday life. When the grandchildren come to visit, they love hearing the stories of when the steel mill was at its peak.

Sneve, Virginia Driving Hawk. *Dancing Teepees: Poems of American Indian Youth.* Illustrated by Stephen Gammell. Holiday, 1989.

This book consists of an illustrated collection of poems, including cradle songs and lullabies, from the oral tradition of American Indians.

AMERICAN INDIAN CULTURE

III THE CHILD'S COMMUNITY

FRIENDSHIPS

Alexander, Martha. **Blackboard Bear.** Dial Book, 1969.

A child's vivid imagination is shown in this appealing story about being too little to play with the other children. The young lad in the story creates his own friend—a large blackboard bear—who magically comes to life.

Alexander, Martha. **My Outrageous Friend Charlie.** Dial Books, 1989.

Jessie Mae admires her outrageous friend Charlie because he can do anything. Charlie keeps telling Jessie Mae that she can be just like him. To help Jessie, Charlie gives her a Super Deluxe Triple Magic kit for her birthday. And in the end Jessie Mae becomes Charlie's "outrageous" friend.

Aliki. **We Are Best Friends.** Greenwillow, 1982.

When Robert's best friend, Peter, moves away, both are unhappy, but they learn they can make new friends and still remain best friends.

Asch, Frank. **Here Comes the Cat!** Illustrated by Vladimir Vagin. Scholastic, 1989.

This book, written in both Russian and English script, is a collaborative effort between a Russian artist and an American author. The story centers on the arrival of a cat in the mouse community. The surprise ending speaks to the young listener about peace and cooperation.

RUSSIAN

Blocksma, Mary. **Manzano! Manzano!** Illustrated by Sandra Cox Kalthoff. Children's Press, 1986.

An apple tree is a friend to all, but it longs for a true friend of its own. This is a translation of *Apple Tree, Apple Tree.*

SPANISH

Butler, Dorothy. **My Brown Bear Barney.** Illustrated by Elizabeth Fuller. Greenwillow, 1989.

The young narrator of this story discusses the various places she visits and the things that she takes with her. Always included on the list is her brown bear, Barney. The book illustrates the concept of relationships at two different levels: interacting with family members and choosing items that go with an activity.

Carlstrom, Nancy White. *Graham Cracker Animals 1-2-3.* Illustrated by John Sandform. Macmillan, 1989.

This collection of poems follows the activities of preschool children as they play, bathe, prepare for bedtime, and explore the world around them. The delightful rhymes help children enjoy the fanciful use of words.

Cohen, Miriam. *Will I Have a Friend?* Illustrated by Lillian Hoban. Macmillan, 1967.

This is the first in a series of three stories about early school experiences and going to kindergarten. Jim feels alone, scared, and anxious until he and Paul become friends. The other books in the series are *Best Friends* and *The New Teacher.*

Fox, Mem. *Wilfrid Gordon McDonald Partridge.* Illustrated by Julie Vivas. Kane Miller, 1985.

To help Miss Nancy find her memory, Wilfrid collects ideas on what a memory actually is and then gathers the things in his life that will help Miss Nancy remember. This is a beautiful story of generations, the elderly, and sharing. This book is available in Spanish.

SPANISH

★ Freeman, Donald. *Dandelion.* Viking, 1964.

When Dandelion receives an invitation to Jennifer Giraffe's tea-and-taffy party, he gets his mane curled and nails manicured; and then he buys a snappy jacket, cap, and walking cane. But Jennifer doesn't recognize him until he gets caught in a cloudburst, loses his hat and curls, and changes back to his "normal" self. Freeman's other books, *Corduroy* and *A Pocket for Corduroy,* are also delightful reading.

★ Galdone, Paul. *The Little Red Hen.* Houghton Mifflin/Clarion, 1973.

This repetitive tale presents the story of the clever little red hen and her three lazy friends. When asked to help with the chores, each friend replies, "Not I." So the little hen teaches them a lesson about helping and cooperating. Other books or retellings by this author include *Jack and the Beanstalk, Puss in Boots, The Teeny-Tiny Woman,* and *The Three Bears.* All of these titles, except *The Teeny-Tiny Woman,* are available in Spanish. Margot Zemach also has a delightful version of *The Little Red Hen.*

SPANISH

Garland, Michael. *My Cousin Katie.* Harper Junior, 1989.

In this beautifully illustrated book, the listener or reader discovers life on the farm and meets young Katie, a farm girl. We follow the farm activities of the day and are introduced to the animals that make their home on the farm.

Gibbons, Gail. *Thanksgiving Day.* Holiday, 1983.

This book presents factual information about the first Thanksgiving and the importance of this holiday for most Americans. The friendship of the Pilgrims and the Indians is discussed as well as the current customs and practices of this holiday. This book is one in a series on traditional American holidays.

Henkes, Kevin. *Chester's Way.* Greenwillow, 1988.

Chester and Wilson, the very best of friends, do not know what to make of their new neighbor, Lilly, who is independent and has a mind of her own. Eventually, Lilly proves herself, and new bonds of friendship are established. But then Victor moves into the neighborhood. The listener is allowed to resolve this "new" problem and bring the story to another happy conclusion. Other delightful stories by this author include *Jessica; Sheila Rae, the Brave;* and *A Weekend with Wendell.*

CHILDREN NEED TO LEARN TO CARE ABOUT OTHERS. AFTER READING STORIES ABOUT FRIENDS, THEY CAN MAKE A PICTURE FOR A FRIEND.

Hilleary, Jane Kopper. *Fletcher and the Great Big Dog.* Illustrated by Richard Brown. Houghton Mifflin, 1988.

When Fletcher encounters the big red dog while riding his Big Wheel around the block, he decides to make a fast getaway and leave the dog behind. Then Fletcher realizes that he is lost and the sky looks quite stormy. The big red dog helps Fletcher find his way back home.

Humphrey, Margo. *The River That Gave Gifts.* Children's Book Press, 1978, 1987.

This is a solid, enjoyable, yet serious story about sharing, giving, and creativity. Four children help care for old people in one African-American community. The author was inspired by the traditional stories and art of West Africa and the Caribbean.

AFRICAN-AMERICAN CULTURE

Hutchins, Pat. *The Doorbell Rang.* Greenwillow, 1986.

Mother has made cookies for Victoria and Sam to share—cookies "as good as Grandma's." But the ringing doorbell brings many friends with whom to share the cookies, until there is only one cookie per child. When the doorbell rings again, Grandma arrives with a whole sheet of cookies for the family.

Kasza, Keiko. *The Wolf's Chicken Stew.* Putnam, 1987.

The wolf in this tale finds the perfect chicken for his chicken stew but decides the stew will be even better if the chicken were a bit fatter. The wolf leaves the chicken all sorts of gourmet delights on her porch. When he claims his "prize," the wolf is surprised by hundreds of small chicks who shower him with kisses and tell him that he is the best cook in the world!

Keller, Holly. *Goodbye, Max.* Greenwillow, 1987.

This is a warm, wise, and reassuring story about loving a pet, losing a pet, and then sharing the grief. The vet had done everything possible, but still, Ben's dog, Max, dies. Ben begins to feel better when he and his friend, Zach, begin remembering funny things Max had done, and they can laugh—and cry—and share memories about Max.

Levinson, Riki. *Watch the Stars Come Out.* Illustrated by Diane Goode. Dutton, 1985.

This story re-creates the journey of two children who are immigrants from the Old World to America at the turn of the century. Their experiences on the voyage and their reactions to New York City are vividly captured in Diane Goode's beautiful illustrations. This book is available in Spanish as *Mira Cómo Salen las Estrellas.*

SPANISH

Lobel, Arnold. *Frog and Toad Together.* Harper Junior, 1972.

Frog and Toad Together is one book in a series of four about two friends who remain friends despite the everyday ups and downs that friendship can bring. The other books in the series are *Days with Frog and Toad, Frog and Toad All Year,* and *Frog and Toad Are Friends* (available in a Spanish translation, *Sapo y Sepo Son Amigos*).

SPANISH

Lyon, George-Ella. *Together.* Illustrated by Vera Rosenberry. Orchard, 1989.

In this illustrated poem about friendship and togetherness, two best friends can dream the same dreams—and sometimes they do. They can even dream their dreams "together."

McKissack, Patricia C. *Mirandy and Brother Wind.* Illustrated by Jerry Pinkney. Knopf, 1988.

Young Mirandy wants to win first prize at the Junior Cakewalk dance. To do this, she attempts to capture the wind as her partner. McKissack and Jerry Pinkney capture a slice of the rural African-American community through words and illustrations. Pinkney has also illustrated Julius Lester's *The Tales of Uncle Remus: The Adventures of Brer Rabbit* and *More Tales of Uncle Remus: Further Adventures of Brer Rabbit, His Friends, Enemies, and Others.*

AFRICAN-AMERICAN CULTURE

Marshall, James. *George and Martha.* Houghton Mifflin, 1972.

Various aspects of friendship are the major themes in this book about two unforgettable hippopotami, George and Martha. They encounter many humorous adventures. George seems to always need some advice or guidance. Martha's wisdom usually gets them through each adventure. Other books in this series include *Back in Town, One Fine Day, Rise and Shine,* and *Tons of Fun.*

Miller, Margaret. *Whose Hat?* Greenwillow, 1988.

In this book the reader is introduced to color photographs of hats and more hats. With each hat, the question is asked, "Whose hat?" Children have the opportunity to guess the occupation of the wearer. Each occupation is illustrated with a grown-up version of the wearer followed by a youthful depiction of children playing the wearer's role.

Minarik, Else Holmelund. *Little Bear.* Illustrated by Maurice Sendak. Harper Junior, 1957.

Little Bear and his considerate friends, Hen, Duck, Cat, and Emily, take part in a series of surprising episodes. This book is also available in a Spanish translation, *Osito.* Other books in the series include *Father Bear Comes Home, A Kiss for Little Bear, Little Bear's Friends,* and *Little Bear's Visit.*

SPANISH

Most, Bernard. *The Cow That Went Oink.* Harcourt Brace Jovanovich, 1990.

A cow that oinks and a pig that moos are ridiculed by the other barnyard animals until each teaches the other a new sound.

Numeroff, Laura Joffe. *If You Give a Mouse a Cookie.* Illustrated by Felicia Bond. Harper Junior, 1985.

In this cycle of events tale, a little boy offers a cookie to a mouse passing by. The mouse then needs a glass of milk, a straw, a napkin, a nap, time to draw, scotch tape, and more. After all this activity, the boy is lovingly exhausted, and the mouse is hungry for another cookie.

Polacco, Patricia. *Rechenka's Eggs.* Putnam, 1988.

When the old Russian lady (babushka) befriends a wounded goose, a special friendship blossoms and grows. When the goose leaves to join the flock, she leaves a very special egg for the babushka. The Ukrainian art of decorating eggs is beautifully illustrated in this touching story. Polacco's other books include *Boatride with Lillian Two-Blossom, Just Plain Fancy, The Keeping Quilt, Thunder Cake,* and *Uncle Vovo's Tree.*

Samuels, Barbara. *Duncan and Dolores.* Macmillan, 1986.

Four-year-old Dolores wants a pet that she can call her very own. Duncan, a four-year-old feline, is up for adoption. Dolores annoys the poor cat and is rebuffed and ignored repeatedly. Dolores is heartbroken and decides to ignore the cat as he ignored her. Her method works!

Shannon, George. *Dance Away!* Illustrated by José Aruego and Ariane Dewey. Greenwillow, 1982.

Rabbit loves to dance all night and day. He always insists that his friends dance with him. They get tired of dancing with Rabbit until, one day, Fox comes along. Rabbit is able to rescue everyone with his dancing.

Surat, Michele Maria. *Angel Child, Dragon Child.* Illustrated by Mai Vo-Dihn. Raintree Publications, 1983.

As a new arrival in an American school, a young Vietnamese girl does not feel welcome or comfortable. She also misses her mother, who was left behind in Vietnam. As she and the other children begin to accept each other and get along, she finds a wonderful surprise.

VIETNAMESE-AMERICAN CULTURE

Varley, Susan. *Badger's Parting Gifts.* Lothrop, 1984.

This story offers a sensitive portrayal of the life and death of a very special friend. Badger's animal friends, feeling overwhelmed by their loss, begin to share warm and loving memories of their friend. These memories represent Badger's lasting gifts to them. It is available in Spanish as *Gracias Tejón.*

SPANISH

★ Waber, Bernard. *Ira Sleeps Over.* Houghton Mifflin, 1973, 1987.

Ira is invited to sleep over at his friend Reggie's house. Because he is sure that Reggie will think he is a "baby," he decides to leave his teddy bear at home. But Ira learns that Reggie, too, needs a teddy bear for companionship and comfort. Another story about Ira is *Ira Says Goodbye.*

Wells, Rosemary. *Peabody.* Dial Books, 1983.

Peabody, the bear, is a special birthday gift to Annie. Her love for him helps him feel real. But Peabody is forgotten when Rita, the talking doll, arrives. Do not miss Wells's other books, including *Hazel's Amazing Mother, Noisy Nora,* and *Shy Charles.*

Williams, Vera B. *Cherries and Cherry Pits.* Greenwillow, 1986.

In this charming story, a little girl loves to tell stories about the colorful pictures she draws. Her stories incorporate family and neighborhood characters in imaginative tales of sharing and giving to one another.

Wolff, Ashley. *Come with Me.* Dutton, 1990.

When a small boy acquires a collie pup, he begins to recount all the wonderful adventures that they are sure to have. Listeners will feel the special bonding between the boy and the dog as well as enjoy the beautiful watercolor illustrations.

Wolkstein, Diane. *The Banza.* Illustrated by Marc Brown. Dial Books, 1981.

After Teegra, the little tiger, and Cabree, a little goat, are lost and find each other, Teegra's family comes for him. Cabree is lonely until Teegra brings him a banza, an instrument like a banjo, to make music from the heart and keep Cabree safe. This Haitian folktale is perfect for sharing with a group of children.

> "DAILY EXPOSURE TO QUALITY LITERATURE CAUSES THE CHILDREN'S READING HABIT TO DEVELOP QUITE NATURALLY AND ENTHUSIASTICALLY."
>
> REGIE ROUTMAN
> *TRANSITIONS FROM LITERATURE TO LITERACY*
> N.D., P. 35

CELEBRATIONS

Asch, Frank. *Happy Birthday, Moon.* Prentice Hall, 1982.

Bear discovers that he and the moon have a birthday on the same day. He decides to give the moon a present—a very special top hat—because that is what he would like also. The ideas of sharing and friendship surface throughout the story as Bear plans his special surprise for the moon.

Baylor, Byrd. *I'm in Charge of Celebrations.* Illustrated by Peter Parnall. Macmillan, 1986.

A desert dweller celebrates a triple rainbow, a chance encounter with a coyote, and other wonders of the wilderness. The story raises awareness of the opportunity for daily celebrations. Other books by this author/illustrator team include *The Best Town in the World; Hawk, I'm Your Brother; If You Are a Hunter of Fossils; The Way to Start a Day;* and *When Clay Bird Sings.*

Brown, Tricia. *Hello, Amigos!* Photographs by Fran Ortiz. Holt, 1986.

Frankie Valdez is a Mexican-American boy who lives in the Mission district of San Francisco. This book tells about a special celebration in his life—his birthday—and the ways that family and friends make the day extra special for Frankie.

MEXICAN-AMERICAN CULTURE

★ Freeman, Donald. *Dandelion.* Viking, 1964.

When Dandelion receives an invitation to Jennifer Giraffe's tea-and-taffy party, he gets his mane curled and nails manicured; and then he buys a snappy jacket, cap, and walking cane. But Jennifer doesn't recognize him until he gets caught in a cloudburst, loses his hat and curls, and changes back to his "normal" self. Freeman's other books, *Corduroy* and *A Pocket for Corduroy,* are also delightful reading.

Gibbons, Gail. *Catch the Wind! All About Kites.* Little, 1989.

In this story the listener is treated to a colorful history of kites and kite making. The author presents the factual information about kites through a simple story format—two children rummaging around a kite shop in search of that "perfect" kite.

Gibbons, Gail. *Thanksgiving Day.* Holiday, 1983.

This book presents factual information about the first Thanksgiving and the importance of this holiday for most Americans. The friendship of the Pilgrims and the Indians is discussed as well as the current customs and practices of this holiday. This book is one in a series on traditional American holidays.

Hutchins, Pat. *Happy Birthday, Sam.* Greenwillow, 1978.

It is Sam's birthday. He is a whole year older but not much bigger. He still cannot reach the light switch or his clothes in the closet or the taps on the sink in the bathroom. But Grandpa sends him a little chair "just the right size" that allows him to solve all those problems.

Polacco, Patricia. *Rechenka's Eggs.* Putnam, 1988.

When the old Russian lady (babushka) befriends a wounded goose, a special friendship blossoms and grows. When the goose leaves to join the flock, she leaves a very special egg for the babushka. The Ukrainian art of decorating eggs is beautifully illustrated in this touching story. Polacco's other books include *Boatride with Lillian Two-Blossom, Just Plain Fancy, The Keeping Quilt, Thunder Cake,* and *Uncle Vovo's Tree.*

Rockwell, Anne. *Bear Child's Book of Special Days.* Dutton, 1989.

The months of the year are featured in Rockwell's informative book about annual special events and holidays. The simple text describes a major activity associated with each month. This book shows the sequence of the calendar and builds the concept of time (e.g., days, weeks, months, and years).

Titherington, Jeanne. *Pumpkin, Pumpkin.* Greenwillow, 1986.

Young Jamie planted a pumpkin seed in the spring. All summer he watched his pumpkin grow—from a tiny sprout to a huge orange pumpkin. By Halloween it was ready to pick and carve. But best of all, inside the pumpkin were seeds. Jamie saves six seeds—to be planted next spring.

Wells, Rosemary. *Max's Chocolate Chicken.* Dial Books, 1989.

When Max and his big sister, Ruby, go on an egg hunt, Max finds acorns, ants, and everything else but eggs.

Wilson, Sarah. *Uncle Albert's Flying Birthday.* Simon and Schuster, 1991.

Jennifer Justine and her brother, William, must take their baths after all when a sleepy baker puts soap powder instead of flour in Uncle Albert's birthday cake. Any child who has ever refused to take a bath will enjoy this bouncy and bubbly adventure.

OUTINGS

Albert, Burton. *Where Does the Trail Lead?* Illustrated by Brian Pinkney. Simon and Schuster, 1991.

With the smell of the sea always in his nostrils, a boy follows an island path through flowers and pine needles, over the dunes, to a reunion with his family. The illustrations depict a black family.

Alexander, Martha. *How My Library Grew, By Dinah.* Wilson, 1983.

Dinah watches as "her" library is built near her house. This small book shows what it is like to visit a library.

Burningham, John. *Mr. Gumpy's Outing.* Holt, 1971.

When Mr. Gumpy takes a boat ride on the river, his little boat becomes more like an ark. Soon the boat is filled with goats, cats, sheep, dogs, chickens, pigs, and children. When a squabble begins, everyone gets wet! A companion story is *Mr. Gumpy's Motor Car.*

Butler, Dorothy. *My Brown Bear Barney.* Illustrated by Elizabeth Fuller. Greenwillow, 1989.

The young narrator of this story discusses the various places she visits and the things that she takes with her. Always included on the list is her brown bear, Barney. The book illustrates the concept of relationships at two different levels: interacting with family members and choosing items that go with an activity.

Caines, Jeannette. *Just Us Women.* Illustrated by Pat Cummings. Harper Junior, 1982.

This story is about relationships and travel. A young girl and her favorite aunt plan an exciting trip by car together. The bonding that they experience makes the trip and the planning worthwhile. The illustrations portray African-Americans.

Crews, Donald. *Freight Train.* Greenwillow, 1978.

The young listener or reader learns visually about the types of cars that you might find on a freight train. Donald Crews incorporates the color words into the text, reinforcing the color concept with colored printing. There is no real story line. The listener simply encounters a train making a journey in which it is " . . . moving . . . moving . . . going . . . going . . . gone."

Crews, Donald. *Harbor.* Greenwillow, 1982.

This colorful book depicts the various kinds of boats that come and go in a busy harbor. Other books by Crews that complement this title about transportation are *Airplane, Freight Train, School Bus,* and *Truck.*

Daly, Niki. *Not So Fast, Songololo.* Macmillan, 1986.

Malusi, whose nickname is Songololo, helps his grandmother, Gogo, travel to the city to go shopping. His hand-me-down tackies (shoes) have holes, and he wishes for some new bright red ones. Vibrant watercolors highlight this South African tale of a boy who likes to do things slowly, in his own way.

AFRICAN CULTURE

Downing, Julie. *White Snow, Blue Feather.* Bradbury, 1989.

A small boy's winter trip into the woods is retold in this simple, descriptive story. The author/illustrator's sense for mood and detail helps capture the excitement of the animals

that the boy encounters. The book portrays a child's wonder with nature. Ezra Jack Keats's *The Snowy Day* is a good companion piece for this book.

★ Flack, Marjorie. ***Angus and the Ducks.*** Doubleday, 1930, 1989.

Angus wants to learn about many things, especially what's behind the long green hedge at the bottom of the garden. One day he gets a chance to find out. Other books in the series include *Angus and the Cat* and *Angus Lost.*

Gibbons, Gail. ***Catch the Wind! All About Kites.*** Little, 1989.

In this story the listener is treated to a colorful history of kites and kite making. The author presents the factual information about kites through a simple story format—two children rummaging around a kite shop in search of that "perfect" kite.

Gibbons, Gail. ***Thanksgiving Day.*** Holiday, 1983.

This book presents factual information about the first Thanksgiving and the importance of this holiday for most Americans. The friendship of the Pilgrims and the Indians is discussed as well as the current customs and practices of this holiday. This book is one in a series on traditional American holidays.

Hilleary, Jane Kopper. ***Fletcher and the Great Big Dog.*** Illustrated by Richard Brown. Houghton Mifflin, 1988.

When Fletcher encounters the big red dog while riding his Big Wheel around the block, he decides to make a fast getaway and leave the dog behind. Then Fletcher realizes that he is lost and the sky looks quite stormy. The big red dog helps Fletcher find his way back home.

Hines, Anna Grossnickle. ***Don't Worry, I'll Find You.*** Dutton, 1986.

Mama decides to go shopping at the mall with young Sarah. Sarah wants her doll to go along, but Mother warns that the doll might get lost. When Sarah becomes lost, she stays put and waits for Mother to find her. Other books by Hines include *Come to the Meadow, Maybe a Band-Aid Will Help,* and *Taste the Raindrops.*

Hofstrand, Mary. ***By the Sea.*** Macmillan, 1989.

A young piglet tells about his adventures with his family when his parents take him to the seashore. He recounts the marvelous things that his family is unable to do at home but manages to do by the sea. The story is told in rhymed verse with old-fashioned illustrations.

Horenstein, Henry. ***Sam Goes Trucking.*** Houghton Mifflin, 1989.

By means of full-color photographs, the author shows us how Sam spends the day with his trucker father in a sixteen-wheeler.

Isadora, Rachel. *City Seen from A to Z.* Greenwillow, 1983.

Scenes of city life are illustrated in this black-and-white alphabet book. From skyscrapers to subways, adults and children participate in the activities of the city scene. The city's diverse social, economic, cultural, and multiethnic aspects of life are well represented.

Jonas, Ann. *Round Trip.* Greenwillow, 1983.

The uniqueness of this book is that it can be read forward and backward, right side up and upside down. The plot line is simple: a family is making a trip to the city and then returning in the evening. Each black-and-white illustrated page becomes a new picture when turned upside down.

Jonas, Ann. *The Trek.* Greenwillow, 1985.

The young narrator encounters all sorts of imaginary wild animals on her daily "trek" to school. Joined on the trek by her helper, another student, they make their way through the desert, over the river, and up the mountain to the school doors—thankful, once again, that they made it! Jonas has concealed animals in the everyday things that a child might see on the way to school.

★ Kennedy, Jimmy. *The Teddy Bears' Picnic.* Illustrated by Alexandra Day. Green Tiger, 1983.

This enchanting picture book is based on an old song that was copyrighted in 1907. The bears put on their costumes and have a very special picnic in the woods. Some editions have a recording of the song by Bing Crosby in the back of the book.

Krementz, Jill. *Taryn Goes to the Dentist.* Crown, 1986.

By means of photographs in board book format, the author describes a little girl's visit to the dentist.

Levinson, Riki. *I Go with My Family to Grandma's.* Illustrated by Diane Goode. Dutton, 1986.

When a reunion is planned at Grandma's house, relatives travel from different parts of the city by different means to arrive for the special occasion. This warm, nurturing book will make children want to share memories of getting together with their friends and relatives.

Lobel, Arnold. *Frog and Toad Together.* Harper Junior, 1972.

Frog and Toad Together is one book in a series of four about two friends who remain friends despite the everyday ups and downs that friendship can bring. The other books in the series are *Days with Frog and Toad, Frog and Toad All Year,* and *Frog and Toad Are Friends* (available in a Spanish translation, *Sapo y Sepo Son Amigos*).

SPANISH

Lobel, Arnold. **On Market Street.** Illustrated by Anita Lobel. Greenwillow, 1981.

This alphabet book transports the listener back in time to a European marketplace where he or she is invited to observe and purchase many wonderful things from *A* to *Z*. Illustrator Anita Lobel has created a special person and item for each letter of the alphabet. An opening rhyme and a concluding verse wrap this alphabet book in one delightful package!

Marshall, James. **George and Martha.** Houghton Mifflin, 1972.

Various aspects of friendship are the major themes in this book about two unforgettable hippopotami, George and Martha. They encounter many humorous adventures. George seems to always need some advice or guidance. Martha's wisdom usually gets them through each adventure. Other books in this series include *Back in Town, One Fine Day, Rise and Shine,* and *Tons of Fun.*

Marshall, Janet Perry. **My Camera: At the Aquarium** and **My Camera: At the Zoo.** Little, 1989.

These two books feature a child's experience with a camera while visiting two favorite spots. Marshall pairs a close-up shot and textual clue with a more conventional picture of the "whole" creature. The accompanying text is simple and in large print.

> "WITH BOOKS ADDED TO THE DAY, YOU CAN BE QUITE CONTENT. WITH BOOKS, YOUR INNER WORLD HAS NO WALLS."
>
> NATALIE BABBITT
> AMERICAN AUTHOR

Merriam, Eve. **Where Is Everybody? An Animal Alphabet.** Illustrated by Diane de Groat. Simon and Schuster, 1989.

This alphabet book has a variety of animals performing everyday activities of humans. Each page is filled with objects that begin with the featured letter. An additional, humorous touch to each page is having the child locate the animal photographer, a mysterious mole that appears throughout the book.

Pfanner, Louise. **Louise Builds a Boat.** Orchard, 1989.

When Louise decides to build a boat, she plans to include many special features, such as a galley to cook in, a figurehead to paint on, and lanterns to light the night sky. A companion book by this author is *Louise Builds a House.*

Rosen, Michael. **We're Going on a Bear Hunt.** Illustrated by Helen Oxenbury. Macmillan, 1989.

This new version of an old tale rhythmically follows a family in search of their quarry, the bear. Rosen has added delightful participation sound effects to his version. When the quarry is found, a return trip is in order, with all the difficulties encountered again.

Rylant, Cynthia. **Mr. Griggs's Work.** Illustrated by Julie Downing. Orchard, 1989.

Mr. Griggs so loves his work at the post office that he thinks of it all the time. This is an interesting portrayal of an older community helper. The amusing illustrations are a plus.

Shaw, Nancy. *Sheep in a Jeep.* Houghton Mifflin, 1986.

> One bright, sunny day a flock of sheep set off for an excursion in a Jeep. But what a ride they have! The rhythmic text and humorous illustrations will delight even the most reluctant toddler in this short adventure story. Listeners will also enjoy *Sheep on a Ship* by this author.

Wolff, Ashley. *Come with Me.* Dutton, 1990.

> When a small boy acquires a collie pup, he begins to recount all the wonderful adventures that they are sure to have. Listeners will feel the special bonding between the boy and the dog as well as enjoy the beautiful watercolor illustrations.

STEPPING OUT . . . NEW ENCOUNTERS

Ahlberg, Allan. *Starting School.* Illustrated by Janet and Allan Ahlberg. Penguin, 1988.

> An unusual approach, with the text and pictures interspersed, takes us through not only the first day of school but the whole first year. It includes a broad ethnic mix of children.

Baer, Gene. *Thump, Thump, Rat-a-Tat-Tat.* Illustrated by Lois Ehlert. Harper Junior, 1989.

> The listener is greeted by a marching band unloading from a bus as the story starts. The band then parades across the wildly colorful pages, becoming louder as it gets nearer and softer as it retreats to board the bus for the trip back home.

Baker, Leslie. *The Third-Story Cat.* Little, 1987.

> Alice, the apartment cat, finds an open window and ventures into the great outdoors. In her "escape" to the park, she encounters some troubles and a helpful friend.

Bang, Molly. *The Paper Crane.* Greenwillow, 1985.

> When a penniless stranger stops at a struggling cafe, he is served a meal and treated as a favored guest by the owner and his son. In return, the stranger gives them a folded paper crane that comes to life and dances at the clap of a hand. The book's illustrations combine paper folding, collage, and watercolors.
>
> JAPANESE CULTURE

Bang, Molly. *Wiley and the Hairy Man.* Macmillan, 1976.

> This story is a retelling of the rural African-American tale of how a young boy and his mother outsmart the "hairy man" of the swamp with the help of the family dog. Both the boy and the mother are portrayed as strong, resourceful characters.
>
> AFRICAN-AMERICAN CULTURE

★ Bemelmans, Ludwig. *Madeline.* Viking, 1939, 1985.

Madeline is a nonconformist in a Paris convent school. Told in rhyme, the story of Madeline's appendicitis becomes an adventure. Other titles in this series include *Madeline's Rescue* and *Madeline and the Bad Hat.*

Breinburg, Petronella. *Shawn Goes to School.* Illustrated by Errol Lloyd. Harper Junior, 1974.

Shawn wants to go to preschool; but the first day is scary, and he cries. Things get better soon, and he begins to enjoy school. The illustrations depict an African-American child.

Caines, Jeannette. *I Need a Lunch Box.* Harper Junior, 1988.

While watching his sister prepare for school, a younger brother decides that he needs to have a lunch box, also. He dreams about having a different colored lunch box for each day of school. On his sister's first day of school, he gets a happy surprise. The illustrations depict an African-American family.

★ Duvoisin, Roger. *Petunia.* Knopf, 1950, 1989.

Petunia, a silly yet lovable goose, feels that by carrying a book around with her and loving it, she will become wise. With great humor, the author describes "pride without wisdom." Petunia then decides to learn how to read. Another book about Petunia and her friends is *Petunia, I Love You.*

★ Flack, Marjorie. *Angus and the Ducks.* Doubleday, 1930, 1989.

Angus wants to learn about many things, especially what's behind the long green hedge at the bottom of the garden. One day he gets a chance to find out. Other books in the series include *Angus and the Cat* and *Angus Lost.*

★ Freeman, Donald. *Dandelion.* Viking, 1964.

When Dandelion receives an invitation to Jennifer Giraffe's tea-and-taffy party, he gets his mane curled and nails manicured; and then he buys a snappy jacket, cap, and walking cane. But Jennifer doesn't recognize him until he gets caught in a cloudburst, loses his hat and curls, and changes back to his "normal" self. Freeman's other books, *Corduroy* and *A Pocket for Corduroy,* are also delightful reading.

Gibbons, Gail. *Catch the Wind! All About Kites.* Little, 1989.

In this story the listener is treated to a colorful history of kites and kite making. The author presents the factual information about kites through a simple story format—two children rummaging around a kite shop in search of that "perfect" kite.

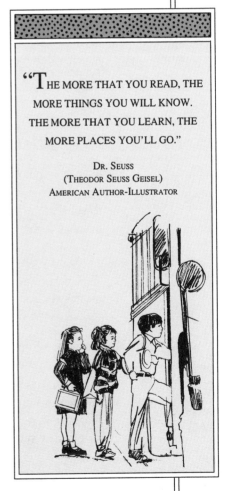

"THE MORE THAT YOU READ, THE MORE THINGS YOU WILL KNOW. THE MORE THAT YOU LEARN, THE MORE PLACES YOU'LL GO."

DR. SEUSS
(THEODOR SEUSS GEISEL)
AMERICAN AUTHOR-ILLUSTRATOR

★ Harper, Wilhelmina. *Gunniwolf.* Dutton, 1918, 1967.

A little girl is warned by her mother to stay away from the jungle because the "gunniwolf" will try to catch her there. One day, while her mother is gone, she goes deep into the jungle picking flowers, and the gunniwolf does catch her! Playful language and dramatic chase scenes highlight this cautionary tale.

Henkes, Kevin. *Chester's Way.* Greenwillow, 1988.

Chester and Wilson, the very best of friends, do not know what to make of their new neighbor, Lilly, who is independent and has a mind of her own. Eventually, Lilly proves herself, and new bonds of friendship are established. But then Victor moves into the neighborhood. The listener is allowed to resolve this "new" problem and bring the story to another happy conclusion. Other delightful stories by this author include *Jessica; Sheila Rae, the Brave;* and *A Weekend with Wendell.*

Hilleary, Jane Kopper. *Fletcher and the Great Big Dog.* Illustrated by Richard Brown. Houghton Mifflin, 1988.

When Fletcher encounters the big red dog while riding his Big Wheel around the block, he decides to make a fast getaway and leave the dog behind. Then Fletcher realizes that he is lost and the sky looks quite stormy. The big red dog helps Fletcher find his way back home.

Horenstein, Henry. *Sam Goes Trucking.* Houghton Mifflin, 1989.

By means of full-color photographs, the author shows us how Sam spends the day with his trucker father in a sixteen-wheeler.

Isadora, Rachel. *City Seen from A to Z.* Greenwillow, 1983.

Scenes of city life are illustrated in this black-and-white alphabet book. From skyscrapers to subways, adults and children participate in the activities of the city scene. The city's diverse social, economic, cultural, and multiethnic aspects of life are well represented.

Johnson, Angela. *Do Like Kyla.* Illustrated by James E. Ransome. Orchard, 1990.

This simple story is about the importance of big sisters and how younger siblings like to mimic all their actions. The reader experiences a day in the life of a young black girl who shows us what it is like to follow the leader.

Kantrowitz, Mildred. *Willy Bear.* Illustrated by Nancy Winslow Parker. Macmillan, 1976.

Getting ready for bed can be a traumatic event for a child. In this story the young boy transfers all of his uneasiness to his bear, Willy. This allows the boy to offer advice and share some worries and fears (e.g., a night-light). Finally, he brings the bear to bed with him so that Willy won't be quite so lonely.

Levine, Ellen. *I Hate English!* Illustrated by Steve Bjorkman. Scholastic, 1989.

A young girl from Hong Kong moves to New York City. She loves her native language and does not want to learn English. With the help of a clever, understanding tutor, Mei Mei learns that she can keep her native language and learn English too!

CHINESE CULTURE

Levinson, Riki. *Watch the Stars Come Out.* Illustrated by Diane Goode. Dutton, 1985.

This story re-creates the journey of two children who are immigrants from the Old World to America at the turn of the century. Their experiences on the voyage and their reactions to New York City are vividly captured in Diane Goode's beautiful illustrations. This book is available in Spanish as *Mira Cómo Salen las Estrellas.*

SPANISH

★ McCloskey, Robert. *Blueberries for Sal.* Viking, 1948.

Sal and her mother go on an excursion to pick blueberries. Sal wanders off and encounters a bear cub. Soon mother and daughter and mother bear and cub cross paths. This is an old story that can be enjoyed by today's readers and listeners.

McKissack, Patricia C. *Flossie and the Fox.* Illustrated by Rachel Isadora. Dial Books, 1986.

Clever, courageous Flossie outsmarts a proud, vain, egg-stealing fox by challenging him to prove that he really is a fox before she will be afraid of him. The text includes African-American dialect from the rural South. McKissack also has written *Mirandy and Brother Wind* and *Nettie Jo's Friends.*

AFRICAN-AMERICAN CULTURE

McKissack, Patricia C. *Mirandy and Brother Wind.* Illustrated by Jerry Pinkney. Knopf, 1988.

Young Mirandy wants to win first prize at the Junior Cakewalk dance. To do this, she attempts to capture the wind as her partner. She overlooks her shy and clumsy special friend, Ezel, who finally triumphs in the end. McKissack and Jerry Pinkney capture a slice of the rural African-American community through words and illustrations. Pinkney has also illustrated Julius Lester's *The Tales of Uncle Remus: The Adventures of Brer Rabbit* and *More Tales of Uncle Remus: Further Adventures of Brer Rabbit, His Friends, Enemies, and Others.*

AFRICAN-AMERICAN CULTURE

★ Marshall, James. *Goldilocks and the Three Bears.* Dial Books, 1988.

In this version of *Goldilocks and the Three Bears*, the listener meets a most unusual bear family. When Goldilocks is discovered, she makes a fast escape and is never seen again by the bears, much to their relief! This story is available in a Spanish version by Maria Claret,

Los Tres Osos. Jan Brett, Lorinda Cauley, Paul Galdone, and Janet Stevens offer additional English versions.

SPANISH

★ Marshall, James. *Red Riding Hood*. Dial Books, 1987.

This cartoonlike version of the famous old German fairy tale is filled with many humorous moments and interpretations. James Marshall has published other fairy-tale renditions: *Cinderella, Goldilocks and the Three Bears, Hansel and Gretel*, and *The Three Little Pigs*. *Cinderella* is retold by Barbara Karlin and illustrated by Marshall. Other versions of *Little Red Riding Hood* have been retold and illustrated by Paul Galdone, Trina Schart Hyman, Beatrice Schenk de Regniers, and Karen Schmidt. Several versions are available in Spanish.

SPANISH

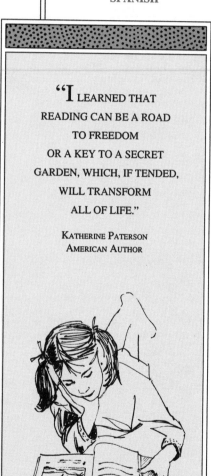

"I LEARNED THAT READING CAN BE A ROAD TO FREEDOM OR A KEY TO A SECRET GARDEN, WHICH, IF TENDED, WILL TRANSFORM ALL OF LIFE."

KATHERINE PATERSON
AMERICAN AUTHOR

Morris, Ann. *Bread, Bread, Bread*. Photographs by Ken Heyman. Lothrop, 1989.

Beautiful photographs capture the commonalities and differences of bread making and bread uses by various cultures around the world. The young listener can observe that the many sizes, shapes, textures, and colors of bread are as varied as the people who eat it.

Morris, Ann. *Hats, Hats, Hats*. Photographs by Ken Heyman. Lothrop, 1989.

Selected photographs of hats give the young listener a multicultural tour around the world. The listener can observe people from many different cultures who use their hats for many different purposes. This author and illustrator also have a multicultural book entitled *Bread, Bread, Bread*.

Oxenbury, Helen. *The Checkup*. Dutton, 1983.

This book is one of many board books and picture books by this author. *The Checkup* is a simple story about a young child's visit to the doctor. Oxenbury's talent of revealing the humorous side of everyday life through simple text and funny illustrations is evident in this selection.

Paek, Min. *Aekyung's Dream*. Children's Press, 1988.

In this tender story, a little Korean girl struggles to adjust to her new life in America.

KOREAN-AMERICAN CULTURE

★ Potter, Beatrix. *The Tale of Peter Rabbit*. Warne, 1903.

In this delightful classic, independent Peter Rabbit disobeys his mother and goes into Mr. McGregor's garden. What follows are almost disastrous consequences. The original Warne editions were reissued in 1987 and are readily available. This book is also available in a Spanish translation, *Pedrín, el Conejo Travieso.* Potter's other books about Peter's relatives and friends are *The Tale of Benjamin Bunny, The Tale of Squirrel Nutkin, The Tale of Tom Kitten,* and so on. David McPhail has also done an illustrated version of *The Tale of Peter Rabbit.*

SPANISH

★ Rey, H. A. *Curious George.* Houghton Mifflin, 1941, 1973.

George, a small monkey, comes to the city from the jungle with the man with the yellow hat because he was so curious about things. His curiosity gets him into many wild situations. This book is also available in a Spanish translation as *Jorge el Curioso.* Two other favorites are *Curious George Gets a Medal* and *Curious George Rides a Bike.*

SPANISH

Rosen, Michael. *We're Going on a Bear Hunt.* Illustrated by Helen Oxenbury. Macmillan, 1989.

This new version of an old tale rhythmically follows the family in search of their quarry, the bear. Rosen has added delightful participation sound effects to his version. When the quarry is found, a return trip is in order, with all the difficulties encountered again.

Schwartz, Amy. *Annabelle Swift, Kindergartner.* Orchard, 1988.

Kindergarten is about to begin, and Annabelle's older sister gives her some hints on how to "do your best" in kindergarten. Unfortunately, her suggestions to her younger sister do not seem to be doing much good. Annabelle's ability to count money, however, saves the day and builds a good feeling about going to kindergarten.

Soya, Kiyoshi. *A House of Leaves.* Illustrated by Akiko Hayashi. Putnam, 1987.

When caught in a rain shower, young Sarah finds shelter under some leaves. She is joined by a number of small creatures. They all happily share the house of leaves. The illustrator, Akiko Hayashi, has collaborated with author Yoriko Tsutsui to produce several other delightful books: *Anna in Charge, Anna's Secret Friend, Anna's Special Present,* and *Before the Picnic.*

Spier, Peter. *People.* Doubleday, 1980.

Spier's detailed illustrations show many differences among people all over the world. Although over five billion people are living on earth, individual differences make each person unique. This book gently reminds us to appreciate those differences through respect for and tolerance of others.

★ Stevens, Janet. *Goldilocks and the Three Bears.* Holiday, 1986.

In this upbeat, modernized version of the old tale about Goldilocks, Papa Bear appears in hiking boots, Mama Bear wears high heels, and Baby Bear wears tennis shoes. A Spanish version of this tale, *Los Tres Osos* by Maria Claret, is available. Other popular versions of the tale are written by Jan Brett, Lorinda Bryan Cauley, Paul Galdone, and James Marshall.

SPANISH

Takeshita, Fumiko. *The Park Bench.* Illustrated by Mamoru Suzuki. Kane Miller, 1989.

The illustrations and the charming story about a bench that is witness to the experiences of different people in a city park will captivate any child's interest. The text in this book is written in English and Japanese.

JAPANESE

Waber, Bernard. *Funny, Funny Lyle.* Houghton Mifflin, 1987.

Lyle, the crocodile, experiences many changes in his life when his mother moves in with the Primm family and Mrs. Primm announces she is expecting a baby.

★ Waber, Bernard. *Ira Sleeps Over.* Houghton Mifflin, 1973, 1987.

Ira is invited to sleep over at his friend Reggie's house. Because he is sure that Reggie will think he is a "baby," he decides to leave his teddy bear at home. But Ira learns that Reggie, too, needs a teddy bear for companionship and comfort. Another story about Ira is *Ira Says Goodbye.*

Young, Ed. *Lon Po Po.* Putnam, 1989.

When a mother leaves her three young daughters alone while she runs an errand, she warns them not to unlock the door for anyone. A very tricky wolf persuades them that he is Grandma and gains entrance to the house. This Chinese version of the Little Red Riding Hood story is illustrated beautifully.

IV
THE CHILD'S WORLD

THE SEASONS AND WEATHER

Aardema, Verna. ***Bringing the Rain to Kapiti Plain.*** Illustrated by Beatriz Vidal. Dial Books, 1981.

This cumulative story poem from Kenya tells how Ki-pat helps end a terrible drought on the African plains. Ki-pat fashions an arrow, pierces the clouds, and loosens the rain. The rich, descriptive language and strong rhythm appeal to young listeners.

AFRICAN CULTURE

Blocksma, Mary. ***Manzano! Manzano!*** Illustrated by Sandra Cox Kalthoff. Children's Press, 1986.

An apple tree is a friend to all, but it longs for a true friend of its own. This is a translation of *Apple Tree, Apple Tree.*

SPANISH

Cooney, Nancy Evans. ***The Umbrella Day.*** Illustrated by Melissa Bay Mathis. Putnam, 1989.

In this fanciful story, young Missy, wearing a bright yellow slicker and scarlet boots and carrying an old black umbrella, starts out in the rain. When it begins to rain harder, Missy starts wishing, and the old umbrella becomes all sorts of imaginative things.

Craft, Ruth. ***The Day of the Rainbow.*** Illustrated by Niki Daly. Penguin, 1989.

Rhythmic verse and shimmering watercolors tell the story of three troubled people on a hot summer day in the city and of the rainbow that brings them together.

Crowe, Robert L. ***Tyler Toad and the Thunder.*** Illustrated by Kay Chorao. Dutton, 1980.

Toad fears thunder, and none of the other animals can comfort him with their fanciful tales of its source. But when the thunder comes again, all the other animals jump into the same hole with Toad. The colorful illustrations depict the various explanations in a cheerful way.

Deming, A. G. ***Who Is Tapping at My Window?*** Illustrated by Monica Wellington. Dutton, 1988.

Told in simple rhymes, this story attempts to answer the question puzzling a young female character in the story—"Who is tapping at my window?" The listener and reader will meet many animals before they discover that the pitter-patter of the rain is tapping at the window.

Downing, Julie. ***White Snow, Blue Feather.*** Bradbury, 1989.

A small boy's winter trip into the woods is retold in this simple, descriptive story. The author/illustrator's sense for mood and detail helps capture the excitement of the animals

that the boy encounters. The book portrays a child's wonder with nature. Ezra Jack Keats's *The Snowy Day* is a good companion piece for this book.

Ets, Marie Hall. ***Gilberto and the Wind.*** Penguin, 1963, 1978.

Gilberto plays with his friend, the wind. The illustrations depict a Latino (or Hispanic) child.

Gibbons, Gail. ***The Seasons of Arnold's Apple Tree.*** Harcourt Brace Jovanovich, 1984.

Arnold's apple tree is his very special place. In this book readers can share the fragrance of its blossoms, the crunch of its fruit, and the gold of its autumn leaves. As the apple tree changes with each season, Arnold also changes the tree in his own special way.

Goennel, Heidi. ***Seasons.*** Little, 1986.

The seasons of the year are shown through the eyes of a child, with great attention to the activities that capture a child's interest. Each season leaves its own special impression—colorful umbrellas in spring, bright pumpkins in the fall, and cheerful snow figures in the winter.

Hidaka, Masako. ***Girl from the Snow Country.*** Translated by Amanda Mayer Stinchecum. Kane-Miller, 1986.

The magic that can be created with a snowfall is portrayed in this story of a little girl in Japan who makes snow bunnies. She journeys with her mother across the snowy fields to the village marketplace.

JAPANESE CULTURE

Hirschi, Ron. ***Winter.*** Illustrated by Thomas D. Mangelsen. Dutton, 1990.

Beautiful photographs of nature capture the cold feeling of winter in this nature book about the season. The simple poem-like text helps build the child's understanding of wintertime survival and adaptation, including migration. A companion book, *Spring,* is also available in this series.

Hoban, Julia. ***Amy Loves the Rain.*** Illustrated by Lillian Hoban. Harper Junior, 1989.

Amy and her mother drive through the rain to pick up Daddy. Luminous chalks capture the rain as we experience it through the few words.

Johnston, Tony. ***Yonder.*** Illustrated by Lloyd Bloom. Dial Books, 1988.

As the plum tree changes in the passing seasons, so do the lives of a three-generation farm family. There is an emphasis on the cycle of seasons in life as well as in nature. This is a lovely book with lots of detail for the eye.

★ Keats, Ezra Jack. ***The Snowy Day.*** Penguin, 1962, 1976.

Peter discovers the delights of playing in the snow. When he attempts to save a snowball in his coat pocket, it melts. He is happy, however, when he discovers the next morning that the snow is still outside. Keats's colorful illustrations instill a sense of wonder and playful excitement for the young reader or listener.

Maass, Robert. ***When Autumn Comes.*** Holt, 1990.

Autumn is a time for making ready and gathering and changing. This delightful picture book, honoring autumn through photography, prepares the listener for the onset of winter.

> I**T WOULD BE A GREAT LEARNING EXPERIENCE TO HAVE CHILDREN BECOME OBSERVANT OF THE WORLD AROUND THEM—THE CHANGING COLORS OF THE LEAVES, THE WARMTH OF THE SUN, THE CHILL OF THE WIND, THE WETNESS OF THE RAIN.**

Martin, Jr., Bill, and John Archambault. ***Listen to the Rain.*** Illustrated by James Endicott. Holt, 1988.

The different moods of rain are depicted in this sensory book about a common element of nature. Through language and illustration, the listener experiences the gentle rain, the singing rain, the pouring rain, and the thundering rain. The authors capture the rain's "mood" through descriptive phrases and rhyme.

My First Look at Home. Random, 1990.

This book is one of a series of sturdy concept books that utilizes actual photographs of items from the child's world and environment. Each item is labeled, and a broader classification is also provided. Common nouns and adjectives are explored in the clear photos. Other titles include *My First Look at Opposites, My First Look at Seasons,* and *My First Look at Touch.*

Parramón, José María. ***La Vida Bajo la Tierra.*** Illustrated by María Rius. Barron, 1986.

This is one of four beautifully illustrated books narrated by animals describing what it is like to live underground, in the air, in the sea, and on the land. The rich descriptive language and illustrations introduce young children to different environments. The other titles are *La Vida en el Aire, La Vida en el Mar,* and *La Vida Sobre la Tierra.* This series is also available in English and English/Chinese.

CHINESE • SPANISH

Parramón, José María, and Asun Balsola. ***La Primavera.*** Barron, 1986.

La Primavera is one of four beautiful books about the seasons of the year. Others in the series are *El Invierno* (summer), *El Otono* (fall), and *El Verano* (winter). *La Primavera* is about spring.

SPANISH

Peters, Lisa Westberg. ***The Sun, the Wind, and the Rain.*** Illustrated by Ted Rand. Holt, 1988.

A side-by-side narration of the earth's making of a mountain and shaping it with sun, wind, and rain is contrasted with a child's efforts at the beach to make a tall sand mountain, which is also affected by the elements.

Ryder, Joanne. *Chipmunk Song.* Illustrated by Lynne Cherry. Lodestar Books, 1987.

The author presents a lyrical description of a chipmunk as it goes about its activities in late summer, prepares for winter, and settles in until spring.

Spier, Peter. *Peter Spier's Rain.* Doubleday, 1982.

This wordless picture book tells about two children and a rainstorm. The children enjoy playing in the rain, but as the wind picks up, they rush home, where it is warm and cozy. Other Spier titles that adults might wish to share with youngsters are *Crash! Bang! Boom!*, *Noah's Ark,* and *Oh, Were They Ever Happy!*

Szilagyi, Mary. *Thunderstorm.* Bradbury, 1985.

When an approaching thunderstorm announces its arrival, a young child rushes home to her mother for security and protection. The little girl experiences various emotions until the storm finally passes.

Tresselt, Alvin. *The Mitten.* Lothrop, 1964.

When a child drops a mitten in the cold, snowy woods, it quickly becomes a home in which some forest animals can keep warm. More and more animals try to push their way in until the mitten can stretch no more. Jan Brett recently has adapted and illustrated another delightful version of this humorous Ukrainian folktale.

Viza, Montserrat. *La Noche.* Illustrated by Irene Bordoy. Barron, 1988.

The beautiful illustrations and interesting text should capture young children's attention. The author describes the activities and changes that take place during the 24 hours of the day. Other titles in the series are *La Mañana, La Tarde,* and *El Anochecer.* The books are also available in English and English/Chinese.

CHINESE • SPANISH

PLANTS AND ANIMALS

Aardema, Verna. *Why Mosquitoes Buzz in People's Ears.* Illustrated by Diane and Leo Dillon. Dial Books, 1975.

This cumulative West African tale begins when the iguana decides not to listen to the mosquito's nonsense, and the story builds until the owl refuses to wake the sun. Another tale by this author and illustrator team is *Who's in Rabbit's House?*

AFRICAN CULTURE

Allen, Pamela. *Fancy That!* Orchard, 1988.

When a brown hen's egg begins to hatch, everyone around has something to say. This familiar story line is told humorously and with playful language.

Barton, Byron. *Dinosaurs, Dinosaurs.* Harper Junior, 1989.

This book is about dinosaurs with horns on their heads; spikes down their backs; and long, long necks. The illustrations are bold, clear, and colorful.

★ Brown, Margaret Wise. *Big Red Barn.* Illustrated by Felicia Bond. Harper Junior, 1989.

This newly illustrated edition of the 1956 rhymed text about farm animals takes the listener through the daily cycle of activities the animals experience. Readers will enjoy the rhymed verse, animal sounds, and reinforcement of color and adjectives. The illustrations depict an African-American family.

Brown, Ruth. *Our Cat Flossie.* Dutton, 1986.

Flossie, the cat, has a very special life with her owners. This cat likes to help around the house, but often her kind of help is not appreciated. Illustrations convey the affection felt for Flossie.

Carle, Eric. *The Grouchy Ladybug.* Harper Junior, 1977.

A grouchy ladybug flies away after an argument with a friendly ladybug. The grouchy ladybug is so upset that he tries to start a fight with every animal he meets. Will the argument ruin his whole day? Carle's other books include *Animals, Animals* (a poetry collection), *The Busy Spider, Do You Want to Be My Friend?* and *The Mixed-Up Chameleon.*

★ Carle, Eric. *The Very Hungry Caterpillar.* Putnam, 1969, 1987.

A very hungry caterpillar eats its way through the pages of this book on its way to becoming a butterfly. The story playfully reinforces the days of the week, different foods, and the life cycle of a caterpillar. This book appears in a Spanish translation as *La Oruga Muy Hambrienta* (1988).

SPANISH

Demi. *Opposites: An Animal Game Book.* Grosset, 1987.

Author/illustrator Demi uses members of the animal kingdom to help illustrate the concept of antonyms, or words that are opposite in meaning. Common adjectives (big/little, old/young) are treated most frequently, although there are some prepositions (over/under), a verb or two (come/go), and several nouns (day/night, circle/square). Short verses or riddles accompany each pair of words.

Deming, A. G. *Who Is Tapping at My Window?* Illustrated by Monica Wellington. Dutton, 1988.

Told in simple rhymes, this story attempts to answer the question puzzling a young female character in the story—"Who is tapping at my window?" The listener and reader will meet many animals before they discover that the pitter-patter of the rain is tapping at the window.

Downing, Julie. *White Snow, Blue Feather.* Bradbury, 1989.

A small boy's winter trip into the woods is retold in this simple, descriptive story. The author/illustrator's sense for mood and detail helps capture the excitement of the animals that the boy encounters. The book portrays a child's wonder with nature. Ezra Jack Keats's *The Snowy Day* is a good companion piece for this book.

Ehlert, Lois. *Feathers for Lunch.* Harcourt Brace Jovanovich, 1990.

This oversized book is actually a primary student's bird identification guide. When an escaped house cat encounters a backyard full of different bird species, the bell around its neck warns the birds that danger is near. The glossary in the back of the book describes the birds that get away.

Ehlert, Lois. *Planting a Rainbow.* Harcourt Brace Jovanovich, 1988.

Planting a yearly garden (by mother and daughter) is the major focus of this story. The book takes the reader through the growing process and closes with a floral tribute to each color of the rainbow. The "rainbow" makes a bouquet that can be picked and brought home.

Fox, Mem. *Hattie and the Fox.* Illustrated by Patricia Mullins. Bradbury, 1987.

When Hattie Hen warns the rest of the barnyard animals about the danger (a fox) she spies in the bush, they do not pay any attention. The repetitive nature of the book's structure makes this an excellent choice for early listeners to experience. This book is available in "big book" format. This author's other books include *Koala Lou* and *Possum Magic.*

Galdone, Paul. *The Three Little Kittens.* Clarion, 1986.

Three little kittens lose, find, soil, and wash their mittens. This favorite Mother Goose rhyme is about these careless kittens who always manage to correct their mistakes.

Garland, Michael. *My Cousin Katie.* Harper Junior, 1989.

In this beautifully illustrated book, the listener or reader discovers life on the farm and meets young Katie, a farm girl. We follow the farm activities of the day and are introduced to the animals that make their home on the farm.

Gibbons, Gail. *The Seasons of Arnold's Apple Tree.* Harcourt Brace Jovanovich, 1984.

Arnold's apple tree is his very special place. In this book readers can share the fragrance of its blossoms, the crunch of its fruit, and the gold of its autumn leaves. As the apple tree changes with each season, Arnold also changes the tree in his own special way.

Ginsburg, Mirra. *Good Morning, Chick.* Illustrated by Byron Barton. Greenwillow, 1980.

When a little chick emerges from its shell, it is ready to begin some of life's adventures. This story tells about a day in the young chick's life. The chick must find food and be protected from the cat. Mother Hen keeps a very watchful eye on the cat.

Hirschi, Ron. *Winter.* Illustrated by Thomas D. Mangelsen. Dutton, 1990.

Beautiful photographs of nature capture the cold feeling of winter in this nature book about the season. The simple poem-like text helps build the child's understanding of wintertime survival and adaptation, including migration. A companion book, *Spring,* is also available in this series.

★ Hutchins, Pat. *Good-Night, Owl!* Macmillan, 1972.

Owl cannot get to sleep during the day with the bees buzzing, the crows cawing, the starlings chittering, and the jays screaming. This humorous, repetitive tale with predictable phrases has an unpredictable ending. This story is available in "big book" format and in Spanish.

SPANISH

★ Ivimey, John W. *The Complete Story of the Three Blind Mice.* Illustrated by Paul Galdone. Houghton Mifflin, 1989.

Three small mice in search of fun become hungry, scared, blind, wise, and finally, happy. Inspired by the chilling lines of the original nursery rhyme, Ivimey has expanded the rodents' tale and given it a happy ending.

Jernigan, Gisela. *One Green Mesquite Tree.* Illustrated by E. Wesley Jernigan. Harbinger, 1988.

The desert environment provides an unusual setting for a counting book. The interaction of desert plants and animal life allows children to develop a deeper understanding of the desert community as they practice counting.

Jonas, Ann. *The Trek.* Greenwillow, 1985.

The young narrator encounters all sorts of imaginary wild animals on her daily "trek" to school. Joined on the trek by her helper, another student, they make their way through the desert, over the river, and up the mountain to the school doors—thankful, once again, that they made it! Jonas has concealed animals in the everyday things that a child might see on the way to school.

Kalan, Robert. *Jump, Frog, Jump!* Illustrated by Byron Barton. Greenwillow, 1981.

In this tale a frog escapes from one close call after another. Young listeners will eagerly root for the frog in this participation story. The compassionate behavior of a little boy adds to the thoughtful message about kindness to animals. Other books by Kalan include *Building a House, Buzz-Buzz-Buzz, Harry Is a Scaredy-Cat, Hester, Wheels,* and *Where's Al?*

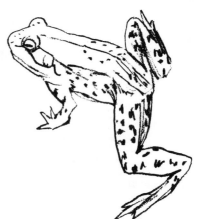

King, Deborah. *Cloudy*. Putnam, 1989.

This book with a simple text describes the way Cloudy, a gray-and-black cat, sometimes spends his day. The listener follows Cloudy on his excursions through nature. Cloudy always returns home to share his adventures with a special friend.

★ Kipling, Rudyard. *The Elephant's Child*. Illustrated by Arlette Lavie. Knopf, 1986.

In this classic tale, the listener meets Kipling's young elephant with the short trunk. The elephant is curious about what the crocodiles have for dinner. This story is one of Kipling's *Just So Stories* that is enjoyable and appealing to the young listener.

★ Krauss, Ruth. *The Carrot Seed*. Illustrated by Crockett Johnson. Harper Junior, 1945, 1989.

A little boy plants a carrot seed. He is sure it will come up, but everyone else is sure it will not. Everyday the boy pulls weeds and sprinkles the ground with water. And then one day, the boy's dream is fulfilled, just as he knew it would be. This book is available in Spanish as *Una Semilla de Zanahoria*.

SPANISH

Lester, Alison. *Imagine*. Houghton Mifflin, 1990.

This book provides a wonderful introduction to the animal world. The bright, lively illustrations are full of things to be discovered and learned.

Lewin, Hugh. *Jafta*. Illustrated by Lisa Kopper. Carolrhoda, 1981.

Jafta, a young African boy, compares some of his everyday moods, feelings, and actions with those of the animals that are a common part of his country and his heritage. Young listeners get a wonderful introduction to the use of similes. Other books in the Jafta series include *Jafta and the Wedding, Jafta's Father, Jafta's Mother,* and *Jafta: The Journey*.

AFRICAN CULTURE

★ Lionni, Leo. *Inch by Inch*. Astor-Honor, 1962.

The inchworm saves his life by telling the hungry robin how useful he is for measuring things. He measures the robin's feathers. The robin is so impressed that he takes his friend to the other birds for measuring. He is even asked to measure the nightingale's song, a task which he does very cleverly. This selection is available in a Spanish translation.

SPANISH

★ Lionni, Leo. *Swimmy*. Pantheon, 1963.

Swimmy, a small fish, encounters a variety of beautiful undersea life after he narrowly escapes the jaws of a big fish. Eventually, he meets some other small fish, and together they form a school of fish large enough to chase the big fish away. This book is available in a Spanish translation, *Nadarín*.

SPANISH

Marshall, Janet Perry. *My Camera: At the Aquarium* and *My Camera: At the Zoo.* Little, 1989.

These two books feature a child's experience with a camera while the child visits two favorite spots. Marshall pairs a close-up shot and textual clue with a more conventional picture of the whole creature. The accompanying simple text in large print is presented as a child would relate reactions and perceptions.

> "EXPOSING CHILDREN TO GOOD LITERATURE, PRESENTED FOR ENJOYMENT, WILL INCREASE THE CHANCES THAT THEIR READING LIFE DOESN'T END WITH HIGH SCHOOL GRADUATION."
>
> MARGARET MARY KIMMEL
> AND ELIZABETH SEGEL
> *FOR READING OUT LOUD! A GUIDE TO SHARING BOOKS WITH CHILDREN*
> N.D., P. 22

Martin, Jr., Bill, and John Archambault. *Here Are My Hands.* Illustrated by Ted Rand. Holt, 1985.

In this delightful concept book, the child learns about the various parts of his or her body through rhymed couplets. Children of different ethnic backgrounds are illustrated in Ted Rand's colorful drawings. The book comes to a logical closure with "And here is my skin that bundles me in."

Marzollo, Jean. *Pretend You're a Cat.* Illustrated by Jerry Pinkney. Dial Books, 1990.

This book's rhyming verses ask the reader to purr like a cat, scratch like a dog, leap like a squirrel, and bark like a seal.

Miller, Jane. *Farm Noises.* Simon and Schuster, 1988.

Stunning color photographs show animals and machines on the farm as the text describes the noises they make. *Farm Alphabet* is another not-to-be-missed book by Jane Miller.

Moore, Inga. *Fifty Red Night-Caps.* Chronicle, 1988.

When the caps that Nico is carrying to market are stolen by some mischievous monkeys as he is napping, Nico must find a way to get them back. Quite accidentally he solves the problem. A companion story to share with this selection is the wonderful classic, *Caps for Sale,* written and illustrated by Esphyr Slobodkina.

O'Donnell, Elizabeth. *I Can't Get My Turtle to Move.* Illustrated by Maxie Chambliss. Morrow Junior, 1989.

This story provides an approach to developing number concepts from one to ten. The narrator is able to get all her animal friends active (three kittens purr, four puppies sit, seven ants march, and so on) except the turtle, which will not move. She finally succeeds—with one magic word.

Ormerod, Jan. *Our Ollie.* Lothrop, 1986.

The first of a series, *Our Ollie* tells of an Asian-American toddler who yawns like a hippo, sleeps like a cat, and is dressed like a parrot. Others in the series are *Silly Goose* and *Young Joe.*

Ormerod, Jan. *Silly Goose.* Lothrop, 1986.

A little girl delights in silliness as she tells all the ways she can move like various animals. This book is part of a series of books about toddlers.

Parramón, José María. *Al Zoo.* Illustrated by G. Sales. Barron, 1990.

Through the vivid illustrations of this book, young children take an interesting field trip through the zoo. This book, from a series of four books called MY FIRST VISIT, introduces children to the animal kingdom. The other titles are *Al Acuario, Al Aviario,* and *A la Granja.* These books are also available in English and English/Chinese.

CHINESE • SPANISH

Pryor, Bonnie. *Greenbrook Farm.* Illustrated by Mark Graham. Simon and Schuster, 1991.

Spring at Greenbrook Farm bursts with the new life of many baby animals, including a calf, a filly, chicks, and ducklings, and a new baby in the family.

Reeves, Mona Rabun. *I Had a Cat.* Illustrated by Julie Downing. Bradbury, 1989.

A young girl with a marvelous imagination tells about all the pets that she has had in her life and how she eventually had to find each of them a home in the zoo, on a farm, or with a friend. The girl found homes for all the animals except her cat, which had a home with her.

Romanova, Natalia. *Once There Was a Tree.* Illustrated by Gennady Spirin. Dial Books, 1985.

This ecology concept book explores how life continues in the stump of a tree as it attracts a variety of insects, plants, and animals (including man). This Russian story beautifully depicts the interrelated aspects of nature.

Rosen, Michael. *We're Going on a Bear Hunt.* Illustrated by Helen Oxenbury. Macmillan, 1989.

This new version of an old tale rhythmically follows the family in search of their quarry, the bear. Rosen has added delightful participation sound effects to his version. When the quarry is found, a return trip is in order, with all the difficulties encountered again.

Ryder, Joanne. *The Snail's Spell.* Illustrated by Lynne Cherry. Penguin, 1988.

The listener is invited to join a small child who imagines what it is like to be a snail. The text and illustrations represent accurate details about the snail family.

Selsam, Millicent, and Joyce Hunt. *Keep Looking!* Illustrated by Normand Chartier. Macmillan, 1989.

It is wintertime! Where did all the animals go? This science concept book discusses winter habitats and animal behaviors and characteristics. Young listeners are treated to a simple text with excellent illustrations that reinforce the text.

★ Slobodkina, Esphyr. *Caps for Sale.* Harper Junior, 1947.

In this children's classic, a tired peddler loses his caps to a treeful of mischievous monkeys. The monkeys eventually return the peddler's caps by imitating his actions. An updated version of this tale is *Fifty Red Night-Caps* by Inga Moore.

Tafuri, Nancy. *Have You Seen My Duckling?* Greenwillow, 1984.

When a duckling disappears, a mother duck and her seven other ducklings swim around the pond looking for it. The listener will enjoy finding the duck on each double-page spread. This concept book works as both a counting book and a game book. Another concept book by this author/illustrator is *Who's Counting?*

Tafuri, Nancy. *Spots, Feathers, and Curly Tails.* Greenwillow, 1988.

Children encounter familiar farm animals in this guessing-game-format book. Clear pictures add to the overall enjoyment for young and old alike. Tafuri's *Have You Seen My Duckling?* and *Junglewalk* are also fun to share with the very young.

Tejima, Keizaburo. *Fox's Dream.* Putnam, 1987.

A solitary fox enjoys the peace of being alone in an ice-coated forest. Then he joins another fox for companionship. The intricate woodcut graphics add to the telling of the simple text. This book is available in Spanish translation as *El Sueño del Zorro*. Other books by Tejima include *Owl Lake* and *Swan Sky*.

SPANISH

Titherington, Jeanne. *Pumpkin, Pumpkin.* Greenwillow, 1986.

Young Jamie planted a pumpkin seed in the spring. All summer he watched his pumpkin grow—from a tiny sprout to a huge orange pumpkin. By Halloween it was ready to pick and carve. But best of all, inside the pumpkin were seeds. Jamie saves six seeds—to be planted next spring.

Tresselt, Alvin. *The Mitten.* Lothrop, 1964.

When a child drops a mitten in the cold, snowy woods, it quickly becomes a home in which some forest animals can keep warm. More and more animals try to push their way in until the mitten can stretch no more. Jan Brett recently has adapted and illustrated another delightful version of this humorous Ukrainian folktale.

Troughton, Joanna. *How the Birds Changed Their Feathers.* Peter Bedrick, 1986.

This colorfully illustrated South American Indian folktale explains how all the birds changed their feathers from simple white to include the many colors of the rainbow. The change occurs as a magical reward for the brave cormorant.

SOUTH AMERICAN INDIAN CULTURE

Turnip: An Old Russian Folktale. Illustrated by Pierr Morgan. Putnam, 1990.

The turnip seed that Dedoushka planted in the spring grows to such an enormous size that he is unable to pull it out of the ground. He gets the help of his entire family: his wife, his daughter, his dog, his cat, and even a field mouse. Young readers will love the repetition of this cumulative folktale.

Van Laan, Nancy. *The Big Fat Worm.* Illustrated by Marisabina Russo. Knopf, 1987.

In this rhythmic read-aloud tale, a chain of events is set in motion when a big fat bird tries to eat a big fat worm.

★ Ward, Lynd. *The Biggest Bear.* Houghton Mifflin, 1952.

When young Johnny befriends a young bear cub, he gains a friend for life. As the cub grows to full size, Johnny tries to return the bear to his forest home, but the bear keeps returning. The happy conclusion to this Caldecott award-winning classic still satisfies young and old readers alike.

Wildsmith, Brian. *Squirrels.* Oxford University Press, 1974, 1987.

Welcome to the world of the squirrel! In this book children discover facts about what squirrels like to eat, where they live, how they use their tails, how they plan and care for their young, and how they spend the winter months. The vibrant illustrations are characteristic of Wildsmith's style.

Williams, Sue. *I Went Walking.* Illustrated by Julie Vivas. Harcourt Brace Jovanovich, 1989.

When a young boy takes a walk, he encounters many colorful animals along the way. They join his excursion in this repetitive, rhythmic text. Julie Vivas's beautiful watercolor illustrations add a very special touch to the book.

Wilner, Isabel. *A Garden Alphabet.* Illustrated by Ashley Wolff. Dutton, 1991.

Told in rhyming verse, this alphabet book illustrates the variety of activities involved with planning and planting a garden. Young readers will expand their knowledge of garden tools and tasks as well as friendly and unfriendly garden animals. Ashley Wolff's drawings add extra enjoyment to the book.

Xiong, Blia. *Nine-in-One, Grr! Grr!* Adapted by Cathy Spagnoli. Illustrated by Nancy Hom. Children's Book Press, 1989.

The author presents a Hmong folktale about why tigers have *one* cub every nine years instead of *nine* cubs every year. Illustrations suggest the traditional Hmong story-cloths, which record history and legends.

HMONG CULTURE

ENVIRONMENTS

Baker, Leslie. *The Third-Story Cat.* Little, 1987.

Alice, the apartment cat, finds an open window and ventures into the great outdoors. In her "escape" to the park, she encounters some troubles and a helpful friend.

Baylor, Byrd. *The Desert Is Theirs.* Illustrated by Peter Parnall. Macmillan, 1986.

The desert and its dwellers are portrayed in this book about the native people of the American Southwest. The listener can experience the close interaction between the desert environment and the community it supports.

Baylor, Byrd. *Everybody Needs a Rock.* Illustrated by Peter Parnall. Macmillan, 1985.

This poetic guide can help us find our own special rock. Once we find our special rock, we can learn its unique qualities and history.

Bowden, Joan Chase. *Why the Tides Ebb and Flow.* Illustrated by Marc Brown. Houghton Mifflin, 1979.

This folk story explains one of the common elements of nature, the ebb and flow of the tide. An old woman bargains with the Sky Spirit for a shelter. In the process of selecting the shelter, she chooses the stone that plugs the hole in the bottom of the sea. The soft black-and-brown illustrations add to the beauty of this African tale.

AFRICAN CULTURE

★ Brown, Margaret Wise. *Big Red Barn.* Illustrated by Felicia Bond. Harper Junior, 1989.

This newly illustrated edition of the 1956 rhymed text about farm animals takes the listener through the daily cycle of activities the animals experience. Readers will enjoy the rhymed verse, animal sounds, and reinforcement of color and adjectives. The illustrations depict an African-American family.

Downing, Julie. *White Snow, Blue Feather.* Bradbury, 1989.

A small boy's winter trip into the woods is retold in this simple, descriptive story. The author/illustrator's sense for mood and detail helps capture the excitement of the animals

that the boy encounters. The book portrays a child's wonder with nature. Ezra Jack Keats's *The Snowy Day* is a good companion piece for this book.

Ehlert, Lois. **Feathers for Lunch.** Harcourt Brace Jovanovich, 1990.

This oversized book is actually a primary student's bird identification guide. When an escaped house cat encounters a backyard full of different bird species, the bell around its neck warns the birds that danger is near. The glossary in the back of the book describes the birds that get away.

Garland, Michael. **My Cousin Katie.** Harper Junior, 1989.

In this beautifully illustrated book, the listener or reader discovers life on the farm and meets young Katie, a farm girl. We follow the farm activities of the day and are introduced to the animals that make their home on the farm.

Goffstein, M. B. **Natural History.** Farrar, 1979.

This book paints a portrait of our world with sadness and joy and a plea for tenderness. Simple, fresh watercolors highlight this small jewel.

Hirschi, Ron. **Winter.** Illustrated by Thomas D. Mangelsen. Dutton, 1990.

Beautiful photographs of nature capture the cold feeling of winter in this nature book about the season. The simple poem-like text helps build the child's understanding of wintertime survival and adaptation, including migration. A companion book, *Spring,* is also available in this series.

Hoban, Tana. **Look Again!** Macmillan, 1971.

This wordless book is a series of black-and-white photographs each viewed through a small window. After the child has guessed what the full picture might be, the page may be turned, revealing the full photograph. Some of Tana Hoban's other exciting concept books are *I Read Signs; I Walk and Read; Is It Red? Is It Yellow? Is It Blue?; Is It Rough? Is It Smooth? Is It Shiny?;* and *Shapes, Shapes, Shapes.*

Hoberman, Mary Ann. **A House Is a House for Me.** Illustrated by Betty Fraser. Viking, 1978.

Full of colorful illustrations, this rhyming concept book describes the different kinds of houses that we have in our world. The book is an excellent vocabulary builder and lends itself to active participation by the listeners.

"CONSIDER THE INTELLECTUAL, SOCIAL, AND EMOTIONAL LEVEL OF YOUR AUDIENCE IN MAKING A READ-ALOUD SELECTION. CHALLENGE THEM, BUT DON'T OVERWHELM THEM."

JIM TRELEASE
THE READ-ALOUD HANDBOOK
1984, P. 68

Hogrogrian, Nonny. *One Fine Day.* Macmillan, 1971.

In this cumulative folktale from Armenia, a sly fox steals milk from an old woman, who cuts off his tail. In order to get the tail back, the fox must complete a series of tasks.

★ Hutchins, Pat. *Good-Night, Owl!* Macmillan, 1972.

Owl cannot get to sleep during the day with the bees buzzing, the crows cawing, the starlings chittering, and the jays screaming. This humorous, repetitive tale with predictable phrases has an unpredictable ending. This story is available in "big book" format and in Spanish.
SPANISH

Jernigan, Gisela. *One Green Mesquite Tree.* Illustrated by E. Wesley Jernigan. Harbinger, 1988.

The desert environment provides an unusual setting for a counting book. The interaction of desert plants and animal life allows children to develop a deeper understanding of the desert community as they practice counting.

Lindbergh, Reeve. *The Midnight Farm.* Illustrated by Susan Jeffers. Dial Book, 1987.

In this counting book with gentle rhymes, a mother and a young child visit a farmyard community and the surrounding area at midnight. Young children will enjoy counting the animals that appear on each page.

Lobel, Arnold. *On Market Street.* Illustrated by Anita Lobel. Greenwillow, 1981.

This alphabet book transports the listener back in time to a European marketplace where he or she is invited to observe and purchase many wonderful things from *A* to *Z*. Illustrator Anita Lobel has created a special person and item for each letter of the alphabet. An opening rhyme and a concluding verse wrap this alphabet book in one delightful package!

Marshall, Janet Perry. *My Camera: At the Aquarium* and *My Camera: At the Zoo.* Little, 1989.

These two books feature a child's experience with a camera while the child visits two favorite spots. Marshall pairs a close-up shot and textual clue with a more conventional picture of the "whole" creature. The accompanying simple text is in large print.

Martin, Jr., Bill, and John Archambault. *Listen to the Rain.* Illustrated by James Endicott. Holt, 1988.

The different moods of rain are depicted in this sensory book about a common element of nature. Through language and illustration, the listener experiences the gentle rain, the singing rain, the pouring rain, and the thundering rain. The authors capture the rain's "mood" through descriptive phrases and rhyme.

My First Look at Home. Random, 1990.

This book is one of a series of concept books that uses actual photographs of items from the child's environment. Each item is labeled, and a broader classification is also provided. Common nouns and adjectives are explored in the clear photos. Other titles include *My First Look at Opposites, My First Look at Seasons,* and *My First Look at Touch.*

★ *Old MacDonald Had a Farm.* Houghton Mifflin, 1989.

In this version of the familiar song, the listener is asked to look through a peephole and guess which animal comes next.

Parramón, José María. *La Vida Bajo la Tierra.* Illustrated by María Rius. Barron, 1986.

This is one of four beautifully illustrated books narrated by animals describing what it is like to live underground, in the air, in the sea, and on the land. The rich descriptive language and illustrations introduce young children to different environments. The other titles are *La Vida en el Aire, La Vida en el Mar,* and *La Vida Sobre la Tierra.* This series is also available in English and English/Chinese.

CHINESE • SPANISH

Parramón, José María, and Carme Sole Vendrell. *La Tierra.* Illustrated by María Rius. Barron, 1986.

La Tierra is one of four excellent books about the elements. Others in the series are *El Aqua* (water), *El Fuego* (fire), and *El Viento* (air). *La Tierra* is about the earth.

SPANISH

Peters, Lisa Westberg. *The Sun, the Wind, and the Rain.* Illustrated by Ted Rand. Holt, 1988.

A side-by-side narration of the earth's making of a mountain and shaping it with sun, wind, and rain is contrasted with a child's efforts at the beach to make a tall sand mountain, which is also affected by the elements.

Radin, Ruth Yaffe. *High in the Mountains.* Illustrated by Ed Young. Macmillan, 1989.

A child and her grandfather experience the mists, meadows, and mountains of the Colorado Rockies. The illustrations are vibrant, abstract, and stunning.

Reeves, Mona Rabun. *I Had a Cat.* Illustrated by Julie Downing. Bradbury, 1989.

A young girl with a marvelous imagination tells about all the pets that she has had in her life and how she eventually had to find each of them a home in the zoo, on a farm, or with a friend. The girl found homes for all the animals except her cat, which has a home with her.

Rius, María, and José María Parramón. *La Ciudad.* Illustrated by María Rius. Barron, 1986.

This is one of four excellent books about habitats. Others in the series are *El Campo* (countryside), *El Mar* (seaside), and *La Montana* (mountain). *La Ciudad* is about the city.
SPANISH

Rosen, Michael. *We're Going on a Bear Hunt.* Illustrated by Helen Oxenbury. Macmillan, 1989.

This new version of an old tale rhythmically follows the family in search of their quarry, the bear. Rosen has added delightful participation sound effects to his version. When the quarry is found, a return trip is in order, with all the difficulties encountered again.

Ryder, Joanne. *Step into the Night.* Illustrated by Dennis Nolan. Macmillan, 1988.

This book combines a haunting text by poet and science writer Joanne Ryder and luminous illustrations by artist Dennis Nolan. Together, they evoke a child's sense of wonder about the natural world, inviting readers and listeners to imagine the diversity of life around them.

Ryder, Joanne. *Under the Moon.* Illustrated by Cheryl Harness. Random, 1989.

Mama Mouse teaches her little mouse how to tell where home is by reminding her of its special smells, sounds, and textures. The book contains detailed drawings of animals, plants, and vistas.

Selsam, Millicent, and Joyce Hunt. *Keep Looking!* Illustrated by Normand Chartier. Macmillan, 1989.

It is wintertime! Where did all the animals go? This science concept book discusses winter habitats and animal behaviors and characteristics. Young listeners are treated to a simple text with excellent illustrations that reinforce it.

Shulevitz, Uri. *Dawn.* Farrar, 1974.

This book about the morning dawn comes from a Chinese poem about an old man and his grandson. As they sleep on the shore by a mountain lake, the coming of the day is portrayed in quiet subtleness.
CHINESE CULTURE

Soya, Kiyoshi. *A House of Leaves.* Illustrated by Akiko Hayashi. Putnam, 1987.

When caught in a rain shower, young Sarah finds shelter under some leaves. She is joined by a number of small creatures, who all happily share the house of leaves. The illustrator, Akiko Hayashi, has collaborated with author Yoriko Tsutsui to produce several other delightful books: *Anna in Charge*, *Anna's Secret Friend*, *Anna's Special Present*, and *Before the Picnic.*

Yolen, Jane. *Owl Moon.* Illustrated by John Schoenherr. Putnam, 1987.

A child and his father go owling at night on a cold, snowy evening. The listener shares the gorgeous moonlit vistas and the descriptions of what is seen and heard on the excursion. The relationship between father and child shows a bond of love and caring.

PATTERNS (COLORS, NUMBERS, SIZES, AND SHAPES)

Agard, John. *The Calypso Alphabet.* Illustrated by Jennifer Bent. Holt, 1989.

Here are 26 exciting words from the Caribbean Islands. From Anancy to Zombie, John Agard's rhythmic, vital poetry evokes calypso sounds while Jennifer Bent's brilliant pictures introduce Caribbean sights.

CARIBBEAN CULTURE

Bucknall, Caroline. *One Bear All Alone: A Counting Book.* Dial Books, 1986.

This counting book features rhymed couplets that describe all sorts of bear antics starting with one bear all alone, sitting by the telephone, to six bears at the shops buying lots of lollipops. Each page in this book is a special treat! Bucknall's other book, *One Bear in the Picture*, deals with Ted Bear's special day at school—picture day!

Charles, Donald. *Cuenta con Gato Galano.* Children's Press, 1982.

This book not only engages young children in developing number concepts but also it motivates them to join in the rhyme and repetition. Other books in the series are *El Año de Gato Galano, El Libro de Ejercicios del Gato Galano,* and *Mira las Formas con Gato Galano.* These titles are also available in English.

SPANISH

Crews, Donald. *Freight Train.* Illustrated by Donald Crews. Greenwillow Books, 1978.

The young listener or reader learns visually about the types of cars that you might find on a freight train. Donald Crews incorporates the color words into the text, reinforcing the color concept with colored printing. There is no real story line. The listener simply encounters a train making a journey in which it is " . . . moving . . . moving . . . going . . . going . . . gone."

Demi. *Opposites: An Animal Game Book.* Grosset, 1987.

Author/illustrator Demi uses members of the animal kingdom to help illustrate the concept of antonyms, or words that are opposite in meaning. Common adjectives (big/little, old/ young) are treated most frequently, although there are some prepositions (over/under), a verb or two (come/go), and several nouns (day/night, circle/square). Short verses or riddles accompany each pair of words. Each illustration also has a problem to be solved by the listener.

Ehlert, Lois. *Color Zoo.* Lippincott, 1989.

This unusual concept book introduces colors and shapes on die-cut pages. As the pages are turned, animal faces are formed when the die-cut pages are placed on the illustrated pages. The curious toddler will enjoy this book.

Ehlert, Lois. *Eating the Alphabet.* Harcourt Brace Jovanovich, 1989.

In a demonstration of fruits and vegetables from *A* to *Z* with Lois Ehlert's colorful watercolor illustrations, the opening page states: "Apple to Zucchini, come take a look. Start eating your way through this alphabet book." For parents and teachers, the glossary at the end of the book describes 75 different fruits and vegetables depicted in the book with some interesting history about the edible items.

Ehlert, Lois. *Planting a Rainbow.* Harcourt Brace Jovanovich, 1988.

Planting a yearly garden (by mother and daughter) is the major focus of this story. The book takes the reader through the growing process and closes with a floral tribute to each color of the rainbow. The "rainbow" makes a bouquet that can be picked and brought home.

Feelings, Muriel. *Jambo Means Hello: A Swahili Alphabet Book.* Illustrated by Tom Feelings. Dial Books, 1974.

This alphabet book describes the people, landscape, and activities of the people in East Africa. Adults as well as children will enjoy this book. A companion book is *Moja Means One,* a counting book.

AFRICAN CULTURE

Feelings, Muriel. *Moja Means One: A Swahili Counting Book.* Illustrated by Tom Feelings. Dial Books, 1971.

This counting book depicts tribal life in East Africa and follows a similar format as the Swahili alphabet book by Tom and Muriel Feelings. Activities and details of day-to-day interaction are incorporated with the tribal counting system.

AFRICAN CULTURE

Feeney, Stephanie. *Hawaii Is a Rainbow.* Illustrated by Jeff Reese and Jill Chen Loui. University of Hawaii Press, 1985.

Vivid, stunning color photographs organized by color groups depict the customs and culture of the Hawaiian people as well as the plant and animal life found on the islands. Specific information about each photograph is presented in the back of the book. This book is a multicultural treat!

Grossman, Virginia. *Ten Little Rabbits.* Illustrated by Sylvia Long. Chronicle Books, 1991.

This counting book is illustrated with rabbits in American Indian costume, depicting traditional customs such as performing rain dances, hunting, and sending smoke signals. The illustrations are beautiful.

Gustafson, Scott. *Animal Orchestra.* Contemporary Books, 1988.

In this counting book (one to ten), the reader or listener is introduced to the instruments found in the orchestra and some very crazy animal characters who are playing the instruments. Children will enjoy finding the animals that they know and recognize, counting the animals on each page, and learning about the orchestra as an extra benefit.

Hadithi, Mwenye. *Greedy Zebra.* Illustrated by Adrienne Kennaway. Little, 1984.

This is a story of how the animals of the world got their color or markings. They find a wonderful cave filled with an assortment of skins and furs and tails and horns. All outfit themselves except greedy Zebra, who is too busy eating. He is left with only some black material. Other titles by this author include *Crafty Chameleon, Hot Hippo,* and *Tricky Tortoise.*

Hoban, Tana. *Of Colors and Things.* Greenwillow, 1989.

A color concept book rather than a story, this book includes a rainbow collection of everyday objects, photographed in vivid color and then grouped in that color category. A cultural color concept book that would complement this one is *Hawaii Is a Rainbow* by Stephanie Feeney.

Hoban, Tana. *Twenty-Six Letters and Ninety-Nine Cents.* Greenwillow, 1987.

Color photographs of letters, numbers, common objects, and coins are used to introduce the alphabet, the counting system, and coinage. This is two books in one; read one, turn the book over, and read the other one.

Hooper, Meredith. *Seven Eggs.* Illustrated by Terry McKenna. Harper Junior, 1985.

This modified counting/science book has a clever twist to it. During a week, one egg hatches each day. Three eggs contain reptiles, and three eggs contain birds. But the seventh egg contains seven chocolate eggs— one for each of the animals and one for the listener.

Jernigan, Gisela. *One Green Mesquite Tree.* Illustrated by E. Wesley Jernigan. Harbinger, 1988.

The desert environment provides an unusual setting for a counting book. The interaction of desert plants and animal life allows children to develop a deeper understanding of the desert community as they practice counting.

YOUNG CHILDREN CAN LEARN TO IDENTIFY COLORS AND NUMBERS AT HOME OR ON A TRIP TO THE GROCERY STORE.

Jonas, Ann. *Color Dance.* Greenwillow, 1989.

Three young dancers carrying scarves of primary colors (red, blue, and yellow) move across the pages, creating a wide variety of colors in this concept book. White, black, and gray are also introduced to show how tints, shades, and hues are created in the color spectrum.

Jonas, Ann. *Holes and Peeks.* Greenwillow, 1984.

A young child is afraid of holes unless they are fixed, plugged, or made smaller. This reassuring book allows the child to peek through holes that are less frightening, such as a buttonhole.

Jonas, Ann. *Round Trip.* Greenwillow, 1983.

The uniqueness of this book is that it can be read forward and backward, right side up and upside down. The plot line is simple: a family is making a trip to the city and then returning in the evening. Each black-and-white illustrated page becomes a new picture when turned upside down.

Konigsburg, E. L. *Samuel Todd's Book of Great Colors.* Macmillan, 1990.

Vivid color illustrations make this color concept book a "new" favorite with toddlers and preschoolers. The brief text introduces a variety of colors and shows where they may be seen. The young listener can observe the bright colors of the pumpkin, carrot, eggplant, and pickle.

★ Lionni, Leo. *Inch by Inch.* Astor-Honor, 1962.

The inchworm saves his life by telling the hungry robin how useful he is for measuring things. He measures the robin's feathers. The robin is so impressed that he takes his friend to the other birds for measuring. He is even asked to measure the nightingale's song, which he does very cleverly. This selection is available in a Spanish translation.

SPANISH

★ Lionni, Leo. *Little Blue and Little Yellow.* Astor-Honor, 1959.

This color concept book tells the story of two friends, blue and yellow, and how these colors blend to form a third color. The story characters are actually bits of torn paper.

Lobel, Arnold. *On Market Street.* Illustrated by Anita Lobel. Greenwillow, 1981.

This alphabet book transports the listener back in time to a European marketplace where he or she is invited to observe and purchase many wonderful things from *A* to *Z*. Illustrator Anita Lobel has created a special person and item for each letter of the alphabet. An opening rhyme and a concluding verse wrap this alphabet book in one delightful package!

★ Martin, Jr., Bill. *Brown Bear, Brown Bear, What Do You See?* Illustrated by Eric Carle. Holt, 1967, 1983.

A variety of unique, colorful animals parade across the pages of this "classic" story by Bill Martin, Jr. The repetitive nature of the simple tale is so predictable that children can easily "read" the text from the picture clues provided. This book is a "model" concept book for reinforcing the color words and for creating similar pattern stories.

My First Look at Home. Random, 1990.

This book is one of a series of sturdy concept books that utilizes actual photographs of items from the child's world and environment. Each item is labeled, and a broader classification is also provided. Other titles include *My First Look at Opposites, My First Look at Seasons,* and *My First Look at Touch.*

O'Donnell, Elizabeth. *I Can't Get My Turtle to Move.* Illustrated by Maxie Chambliss. Morrow Junior, 1989.

This story provides an approach to developing number concepts from one to ten. The narrator is able to get all her animal friends active (three kittens purr, four puppies sit, seven ants march, and so on) except the turtle, which will not move. Finally she succeeds—with one magic word.

Ormerod, Jan. *Young Joe.* Lothrop, 1986.

This simple counting book has clear, colorful illustrations. Young Joe counts with his fingers as he thinks of familiar animals to count. At the end of the counting, one of the ten puppies that he has counted chooses him.

Peek, Merle. *Mary Wore Her Red Dress, and Henry Wore His Green Sneakers.* Clarion, 1985, 1988.

Each of Katy Bear's animal friends wears a different color of clothing to her birthday party. The illustrations are colorful.

Rockwell, Anne. *Bear Child's Book of Special Days.* Dutton, 1989.

The months of the year are featured in Rockwell's informative book about annual special events and holidays. The simple text describes a major activity associated with each month. This book shows the sequence of the calendar and builds the concept of time (e.g., days, weeks, months, and years).

Shelby, Anne. *Potluck.* Illustrated by Irene Trivas. Orchard, 1991.

At a potluck everyone brings some favorite thing to eat. Alpha and Betty and all their friends (Acton to Zelda) bring appropriate alphabetical food (asparagus soup to zucchini casserole). The illustrations depict children from many ethnic groups.

Stinson, Kathy. *Red Is Best.* Illustrated by Robin Baird Lewis. Firefly, 1982.

The young narrator of this book has one message, "Red is best!" When she paints, painting with red makes her heart sing. This is a delightful adventure with color, envisioned through a young girl's wonderful imagination. The illustrations add the right touch of humor to the clever text. It is available in "big book" format and in Spanish as *El Rojo Es el Mejor.*

SPANISH

Walsh, Ellen. *Mouse Paint.* Harcourt Brace Jovanovich, 1989.

Three white mice discover three bottles of colored paint—red, yellow, and blue. As one little mouse runs through the red paint and then the yellow paint, we discover a trail of orange. Soon the three mice are experimenting with other wonderful color combinations!

Williams, Sue. *I Went Walking.* Illustrated by Julie Vivas. Harcourt Brace Jovanovich, 1989.

When a young boy takes a walk, he encounters many colorful animals along the way. They join his excursion in this repetitive, rhythmic text. Julie Vivas's beautiful watercolor illustrations add a very special touch to the book.

Wylie, Joanne. *Un Cuento de un Pez Grande.* Illustrated by David G. Wylie. Children's Press, 1984.

In this big-fish story, children enjoy the comparison of sizes of different colorful fish through the captivating language and illustrations. Other books in this series are *Un Cuento Curioso de Colores* and *Un Cuento de Peces, Mas o Menos.* These titles are also available in English.

SPANISH

APPENDIX

CRITERIA FOR SELECTION OF LITERATURE INCLUDED IN *READ TO ME*

The following criteria for book selection are offered to help in the choosing of literature to be read aloud to young children. The committee members hope that the books selected for this publication offer illustrative rather than definitive examples that not only invite an engaging shared experience of literature and language but also provide the substance for extended activities and conversation about important themes in a child's life.

The three major areas of consideration that guided the members of the selection committee were the (1) literary qualities of the story; (2) qualities that appeal to a child; and (3) educational potential of the book.

Literary Qualities of the Story

1. Themes of Value

   - Universal, "living" themes that are ageless and timeless
   - Stories that offer a strong beginning, middle, and end, with closure provided by a satisfying ending
   - Themes that are inviting, varied, and creative

2. Illustrations

   - Match the story, work together, and are consistent with the words and story line.
   - Are nonsexist and nonracist (nonstereotyped, well-balanced images).
   - Stir the feelings and imagination of the child.
   - Present different types of creative techniques for illustrations.

3. Language

   - Relevant, natural, direct, familiar language that comes from a child's experience and builds on a child's prior knowledge
   - Powerful, beautiful, varied, and enriching
   - Rich in sound and imagery, with an artful rhythm
   - Nonsexist and nonracist (nonstereotyped, well-balanced images)
   - Characterized by use of new words and fresh presentation in the story
   - Inviting, delightful, and playful

4. Clear Literary Structure

   - Clear plot or story line
   - Believable, realistic story characters
   - Realistic problems and solutions

Qualities That Appeal to a Child

1. Story Appeal

   - Reaches out to all the senses, helping children to imagine the sight, sound, feel, or smell
   - Follows natural interests and developmental issues of the young child
   - Presents facts simply and clearly without too many words
   - Contains delightful and playful language and illustrations
   - Allows a child to identify with the story, character, or events of the story

2. Personal Appeal

   - Varied representation of authors; e.g., gender, ethnicity, or age
   - Variety of multicultural and multilingual folktales and stories
   - Variety of settings and socioeconomic levels
   - Believable characters
   - Variety of formats of book presentation; e.g., book size, picture books, word lists, or pop-up books

Educational Potential of the Book

1. Considerations for Teaching and Learning

   - Selections that are personally appropriate to the interests and experiences of the individual adult and child sharing the experience
   - Themes that lend themselves to reading aloud or storytelling again and again
   - Topics or concepts that are springboards for discussion, discovery, and investigation
   - Substantial content that allows for extending educational activities and integration of various classroom curriculum activities if desired
   - Factual information that is accurate, clear, and concise
   - Photographs and illustrations that are effective and stimulating

2. Production Value

   - Well constructed and sturdy for use by children
   - Currently accessible to the public in libraries and bookstores
   - Varied formats; e.g., size of books, picture storybooks, or board books

RESOURCES FOR ADULTS

The following list of resources for adults is representative. Users of the document may wish to insert other resources that are helpful in their work with young children.

Selected References

Adventuring with Books: A Booklist for Pre-K Through Grade 6. Edited by Mary Jett-Simpson. Urbana, Ill.: National Council of Teachers of English, 1989.

Bauer, Caroline Feller. *Handbook for Storytellers*. Chicago: American Library Association, 1977.

Bauer, Caroline Feller. *Presenting Reader's Theater: Plays and Poems to Read Aloud*. Bronx, N.Y.: H.W. Wilson, 1987.

Becoming a Nation of Readers. Prepared by Richard C. Anderson and others. Washington, D.C.: The National Institute of Education, U.S. Department of Education, 1984.

Books Without Bias Through Indian Eyes (Second edition). Introduction by Beverly Slapin and Doris Seale. Berkeley: Oyate; Oakland, Calif.: Inkworks Press, 1988.

Brenner, Barbara, and others. *Choosing Books for Children: How to Choose the Right Book for the Right Child at the Right Time*. New York: Ballantine Books, Inc., 1986.

Calkins, Lucy McCormick. *Lessons from a Child: On the Teaching and Learning of Writing*. Portsmouth, N.H.: Heinemann Educational Books, Inc., 1983.

Cascardi, Andrea E. *Good Books to Grow On: A Guide to Building Your Child's Library from Birth to Age Five*. New York: Warner Books, Inc., 1985.

Celebrating the National Reading Initiative. Sacramento: California Department of Education, 1988.

Children's Literature in the Classroom: Weaving Charlotte's Web. Edited by Janet Hickman and Bernice E. Cullinan. Norwood, Mass.: Christopher-Gordon Publications, Inc., 1989.

Children's Literature in the Reading Program. Edited by Bernice E. Cullinan. Newark, Del.: International Reading Association, 1987.

Classics to Read Aloud to Your Children. Selected by William F. Russell. Southbridge, Mass.: Crown Publications, Inc., 1984.

Collected Perspectives: Choosing and Using Books for the Classroom. Edited by Hughes Moir, Melissa Cain, and Leslie Prosak-Beres. Norwood, Mass.: Christopher-Gordon Publications, Inc., 1990.

Copperman, Paul. *Taking Books to Heart: How to Develop a Love of Reading in Your Child, For Parents of Children Two to Nine*. Menlo Park, Calif.: Addison-Wesley Publishing Company, Inc., 1986.

Goodman, Kenneth. *What's Whole in Whole Language? A Parent/Teacher Guide to*

Children's Learning. Portsmouth, N.H.: Heinemann Educational Books, Inc., 1986.

Harste, Jerome C.; Carolyn L. Burke; and Virginia A. Woodward. *Language Stories and Literacy Lessons*. Portsmouth, N.H.: Heinemann Educational Books, Inc., 1984.

Ideas and Insights: Language Arts in the Elementary School. Edited by Dorothy J. Watson. Urbana, Ill.: National Council of Teachers of English, 1987.

Kimmel, Margaret Mary, and Elizabeth Segel. *For Reading Out Loud!* New York: Dell Publishing Co., Inc., 1991.

Landsberg, Michele. *Reading for the Love of It*. Englewood Cliffs, N.J.: Prentice Hall Press, 1987.

Lanes, Selma G. *Down the Rabbit Hole: Adventures and Misadventures in the Realm of Children's Literature*. New York: Atheneum, 1971.

Learning to Love Literature: Preschool Through Grade 3. Edited by Linda Leonard Lamme. Urbana, Ill.: National Council of Teachers of English, 1981.

Lima, Carolyn W., and John A. Lima. *A to Zoo: Subject Access to Children's Picture Books*. New Providence, N.J.: R.R. Bowker, 1989.

Lipson, Eden Ross. *The New York Times Parent's Guide to the Best Books for Children*. New York: Random House, Times Books, 1988.

Literature and Young Children. Edited by Bernice E. Cullinan and Carolyn W. Carmichael. Urbana, Ill.: National Council of Teachers of English, 1977.

Lukens, Rebecca J. *A Critical Handbook of Children's Literature* (Third edition). Glenview, Ill.: Scott, Foresman and Co., 1986.

Nevarez, Sandra; Norma Ramirez; and Raquel Mireles. *Experiences with Literature: A Thematic Whole Language Model for the K-3 Bilingual Classroom*. Menlo Park, Calif.: Addison-Wesley Publications, 1990.

Routman, Regie. *Invitations: Changing as Teachers and Learners, K–12*. Portsmouth, N.H.: Heinemann Educational Books, Inc., 1991.

Stott, Jon C. *Children's Literature from A to Z: A Guide for Parents and Teachers*. New York: McGraw-Hill Publishing Company, 1984.

Teaching Multicultural Literature in Grades K–8. Edited by Violet J. Harris. Norwood, Mass.: Christopher-Gordon Publishers, Inc., 1992.

Trelease, Jim. *The Read-Aloud Handbook*. New York: Viking Penguin, 1988.

Whole Language: Theory in Use. Edited by Judith M. Newman. Portsmouth, N.H.: Heinemann Educational Books, Inc., 1985.

Resources for Publications and Instructional Materials

Bilingual Educational Services, Inc.
2514 South Grand Avenue
Los Angeles, CA 90007
(213) 749-6213; fax: (213) 749-1820

Black Oak Books
1491 Shattuck Avenue
Berkeley, CA 94709
(510) 486-0698 or (510) 486-0699

The Children's Advocate (Bi-monthly
    newspaper)
Action Alliance for Children
1201 Martin Luther King, Jr., Way
Oakland, CA 94612
(510) 444-7136; fax: (510) 444-7138

Chinaberry Book Service
2780 Via Orange Way, Suite B
Spring Valley, CA 91978
(619) 670-5200; fax: (619) 670-5203

Claudia's Caravan (Multicultural resources)
P.O. Box 1582
Alameda, CA 94501
(510) 521-7871; fax: (510) 769-6230

Greenshower Corporation
(Multicultural resources; materials in
    languages other than English)
800 N. Grand Avenue
Covina, CA 91724
(818) 859-3133; fax: (818) 859-3136

Hamel-Spanish Book Corporation
10977 Santa Monica Boulevard
Los Angeles, CA 90025
(310) 475-0453; fax: (310) 473-6132

The Horn Book, Inc.
14 Beacon Street
Boston, MA 02108

Iaconi Book Imports
1110 Mariposa Avenue
San Francisco, CA 94107
(415) 255-8193; fax: (415) 255-8742

Lectorum Publications, Inc.
137 West 14th Street
New York, NY 10011
(212) 929-2833; fax: (212) 727-3035

Liberia El Dia
R. Sanchez Taboada 61-A
Tijuana, Baja California
Telephone: 84-09-08

Music for Little People
P.O. Box 1460
1144 Redway Drive
Redway, CA 95560
(707) 923-3991; fax: (707) 923-3241

The Pocket Book (Integrating the primary
    curriculum through themes)
P.O. Box 3143
Livermore, CA 94550

The White Rabbit Children's Books
7755 Girard Avenue
La Jolla, CA 92037
(619) 454-3518

INDEX OF TITLES

A

B

C

H

Happy Birthday, Moon   25, 68
Happy Birthday, Sam   9, 40, 69
Harbor   70
Harriet's Recital   8, 32
Hats, Hats, Hats   55, 78
Hattie and the Fox   3, 19, 87
Have You Seen My Duckling?   5, 92
Hawaii Is a Rainbow   100
Hello, Amigos!   48, 68
Here Are My Hands   22, 90
Here Comes the Cat!   62
High in the Mountains   97
Holes and Peeks   33, 102
Home Place   38, 56
Honey, I Love And Other Love Poems   48
House Is a House for Me, A   56, 95
House of Leaves, A   11, 79, 98
House on Maple Street, The   56, 60
How Do I Put It On?   6, 12
How My Library Grew, By Dinah   70
How the Birds Changed Their Feathers   93
How the Ox Star Fell from Heaven   32, 53
Humphrey's Bear   44
Hush, Little Baby   52

I

I Can't Get My Turtle to Move   4, 90, 103
I Go with My Family to Grandma's   41, 72
I Had a Cat   91, 97
I Hate English!   10, 77
I Hear   4
I Love You, Mouse   26
I Need a Lunch Box   37, 75
I Unpacked My Grandmother's Trunk   20, 27
I Went Walking   23, 93, 104
If You Give a Mouse a Cookie   66
I'll Always Love You   34, 45
Imagine   89
I'm in Charge of Celebrations   68
In the Forest   26
Inch by Inch   89, 102
Ira Sleeps Over   67, 80

Is Your Mama a Llama?   20, 39
It Could Always Be Worse: A Yiddish
   Folktale   57

J

Jafta   14, 21, 89
Jamaica's Find   13
Jambo Means Hello: A Swahili Alphabet
   Book   100
Jennie's Hat   54
Jesse Bear, What Will You Wear?   3, 8
Journey Cake, Ho!   54
Judge Rabbit and the Tree Spirit   30
Jump, Frog, Jump!   88
Just Like Jasper!   2, 8
Just Us Women   37, 70

K

Keep Looking!   92, 98
Keeping Quilt, The   42, 60
Kevin's Grandma   45
King Bidgood's in the Bathtub   51
Koala Lou, I'll Always Love You   39
Kweeks of Kookatumdee, The   15, 33, 53

L

Lady with the Alligator Purse, The   23, 31
Leo the Late Bloomer   10, 41, 49
Like Me   8
Line Up Book, The   50
Listen to the Rain   84, 96
Little Bear   66
Little Blue and Little Yellow   102
Little Engine That Could, The   15
Little House of Your Own, A   26
Little Red Hen, The   9, 63
Lizard's Song   11, 29, 57
Lon Po Po   80
Look Again!   95
Louise Builds a Boat   73
Loving   60

M

N

O

P

Index of Authors

A

Aardema, Verna   82, 85
Ackerman, Karen   36
Ada, Alma Flor   17
Adler, David A.   57
Adoff, Arnold   36
Agard, John   99
Ahlberg, Allan   17, 74
Albert, Burton   36, 69
Alexander, Martha   7, 24, 36, 62, 70
Aliki   7, 36, 58, 62
Allen, Jeffrey   7, 12, 47
Allen, Pamela   2, 85
Anderson, Peggy Perry   47
Archambault, John   22, 84, 90, 96
Arnold, Tedd   24, 47
Asch, Frank   24, 25, 62, 68

B

Baer, Gene   2, 18, 74
Baker, Keith   7
Baker, Leslie   74, 94
Balsola, Asun   84
Bang, Molly   47, 74
Barton, Byron   86
Baum, Louis   36
Bayer, Jane   18
Baylor, Byrd   68, 94
Bemelmans, Ludwig   7, 75
Berger, Barbara   25
Blaustein, Muriel   12, 36
Blocksma, Mary   25, 62, 82
Blood, Charles L.   58
Bowden, Joan Chase   94
Breinburg, Petronella   7, 31, 75
Brightman, Alan   8
Brown, Margaret Wise   18, 25, 37, 48,
   86, 94

Brown, Ruth   86
Brown, Tricia   48, 68
Browne, Anthony   2, 48
Bucknall, Caroline   2, 18, 99
Bunting, Eve   37
Burningham, John   2, 25, 70
Butler, Dorothy   37, 62, 70
Butterworth, Nick   2, 8

C

Caines, Jeannette   37, 70, 75
Carle, Eric   32, 52, 86
Carlson, Nancy   8, 32
Carlstrom, Nancy White   3, 8, 63
Cazet, Denys   48
Charles, Donald   99
Charlip, Remy   18
Chorao, Kay   3
Clifton, Lucille   32, 37
Cohen, Barbara   38, 58
Cohen, Miriam   32, 63
Cooney, Barbara   3, 18
Cooney, Nancy Evans   25, 82
Craft, Ruth   48, 82
Crews, Donald   70, 99
Crowe, Robert L.   12, 32, 82

D

Daly, Niki   54, 70
De Paola, Tomie   3, 8, 19, 25, 38, 52,
   54, 58
De Regniers, Beatrice Schenk   3, 19, 26
Delacre, Lulu   18
Demi   8, 19, 86, 99
Deming, A. G.   19, 82, 86
Downing, Julie   70, 82, 87, 94
Dragonwagon, Crescent   38, 52, 56
Duvoisin, Roger   26, 75

Index of Illustrators and Photographers

Knight, Hilary   20
Konigsburg, E. L.   102
Kopper, Lisa   14, 21, 89
Krauss, Ruth   21, 56
Krementz, Jill   4, 72

L

Langley, Jonathan   11, 16
Lasker, Joe   11, 43
Lavallee, Barbara   13
Lavie, Arlette   89
Lent, Blair   29, 53
Lester, Alison   28, 89
Lewis, Robin Baird   11, 103
Lionni, Leo   14, 89, 102
Lloyd, Errol   7, 31, 75
Lobel, Anita   20, 46, 55, 73, 96, 102
Lobel, Arnold   41, 49, 65, 72
Lofts, Pamela   39
Lomas Garza, Carmen   59
Long, Sylvia   101
Luzak, Dennis   59

M

McCloskey, Robert   53, 54, 77
McCully, Emily   36
McDermott, Gerald   14, 59
McKenna, Terry   101
McMillan, Bruce   21, 28
McPhail, David   10, 15, 21, 49
Maass, Robert   84
Mangelsen, Thomas D.   83, 88, 95
Marshall, James   7, 12, 28, 29, 42, 47, 56, 65,
   73, 78
Marshall, Janet Perry   73, 90, 96
Martchenko, Michael   15
Mathis, Melissa Bay   25, 82
Mayer, Mercer   33, 50
Miller, Margaret   54, 65
Miller, Jane   90
Moore, Inga   55, 90

Morgan, Pierr   54, 93
Most, Bernard   10, 66
Mullins, Patricia   3, 19, 87
Munoz, Rie   15, 55
Murphy, Jill   42, 50

N

Nolan, Dennis   98

O

O'Brien, Anne Sibley   13
Ohtomo, Yasuo   5, 6, 11, 12, 44
Ormerod, Jan   4, 10, 48, 90, 91, 103
Ortiz, Fran   48, 68
Oxenbury, Helen   4, 5, 43, 50, 73, 78, 79, 91, 98

P

Paek, Min   10, 78
Parker, Nancy Winslow   13, 33, 46, 51, 58, 76
Parnall, Peter   68, 94
Parramón, José M.   84
Peck, Beth   56, 60
Peek, Merle   23, 55, 103
Peet, Bill   15, 33, 53
Pfanner, Louise   73
Pincus, Harriet   43, 50
Pinkney, Brian   36, 69
Pinkney, Jerry   22, 38, 56, 58, 65, 77, 90
Polacco, Patricia   42, 60, 66, 69
Potter, Beatrix   78
Potter, Katherine   42, 59

R

Rand, Ted   22, 84, 90, 97
Ransome, James E.   40, 76
Rawlins, Donna   42
Reese, Jeff   100

PUBLICATIONS AVAILABLE FROM THE DEPARTMENT OF EDUCATION

This publication is one of over 600 that are available from the California Department of Education. Some of those that may be of special interest to readers of this publication are the following:

CHILD DEVELOPMENT

ISBN	Title (Date of publication)	Price
0-8011-0883-7	The Ages of Infancy: Caring for Young, Mobile, and Older Infants (videocassette and guide) (1990)*	$65.00
0-8011-1017-3	California State Plan for the Child Care and Development Services Funded Under Federal Block Grant (1991)	4.75
0-8011-1011-3	Exemplary Program Standards for Child Care Development Programs Serving Preschool and School-Age Children (1991)	3.50
0-8011-0751-2	First Moves: Welcoming a Child to a New Caregiving Setting (videocassette and guide) (1988)*	65.00
0-8011-0839-x	Flexible, Fearful, or Feisty: The Different Temperaments of Infants and Toddlers (videocassette and guide) (1990)*	65.00
0-8011-0809-8	Getting In Tune: Creating Nurturing Relationships with Infants and Toddlers (videocassette and guide) (1990)*	65.00
0-8011-0734-2	Here They Come: Ready or Not—Report of the School Readiness Task Force (Full Report) (1988)	4.25
0-8011-0750-4	Infant/Toddler Caregiving: An Annotated Guide to Media Training Materials (1989)	8.75
0-8011-0878-0	Infant/Toddler Caregiving: A Guide to Creating Partnerships with Parents (1990)	8.25
0-8011-0880-2	Infant/Toddler Caregiving: A Guide to Language Development and Communication (1991)	8.25
0-8011-0877-2	Infant/Toddler Caregiving: A Guide to Routines (1990)	8.25
0-8011-0879-9	Infant/Toddler Caregiving: A Guide to Setting Up Environments (1990)	8.25
0-8011-0876-4	Infant/Toddler Caregiving: A Guide to Social–Emotional Growth and Socialization (1990)	8.25
0-8011-0869-1	It's Not Just Routine: Feeding, Diapering, and Napping Infants and Toddlers (videocassette and guide) (1990)*	65.00
0-8011-0753-9	Respectfully Yours: Magda Gerber's Approach to Professional Infant/Toddler Care (videocassette and guide) (1988)*	65.00
0-8011-0752-0	Space to Grow: Creating a Child Care Environment for Infants and Toddlers (videocassette and guide) (1988)*	65.00
0-8011-0758-x	Visions for Infant/Toddler Care: Guidelines for Professional Caregiving (1989)	5.50

LANGUAGE AND LITERATURE

ISBN	Title (Date of publication)	Price
0-8011-0760-1	Celebrating the National Reading Initiative (1989)	$6.75
0-8011-0796-2	Effective Language Arts Programs for Chapter 1 and Migrant Education Students (1989)	4.25
0-8011-0041-0	English–Language Arts Framework for California Public Schools (1987)	3.75
0-8011-0732-8	English–Language Arts Model Curriculum Guide, K–8 (1988)	3.75
0-8011-0892-6	Literature for History–Social Science, Kindergarten Through Grade Eight (1991)	5.25
0-8011-0979-5	Readings for the Christopher Columbus Quincentenary (1992)	2.75†
0-8011-0745-8	Recommended Readings in Literature, Kindergarten Through Grade Eight, Annotated Edition (1988)‡	4.50
0-8011-0895-0	Recommended Readings in Spanish Literature: Kindergarten Through Grade Eight (1991)	3.25

*Videocassette also available in Chinese (Cantonese) and Spanish at the same price.
†Also available in quantities of 10 for $7.50 (item number 9875); 30 for $20 (9876); and 100 for $60 (9877).
‡Includes *Addendum* (ISBN 0-8011-0863-2).

MATERIALS FOR PARENTS

ISBN	Title (Date of publication)	Price
0-8011-1036-x	California Strategic Plan for Parental Involvement in Education (1992)	$5.00
0-8011-0874-8	The Changing History–Social Science Curriculum: A Booklet for Parents (1990)	10/5.00*
0-8011-0867-5	The Changing Language Arts Curriculum: A Booklet for Parents (1990)	10/5.00*
0-8011-0928-0	The Changing Language Arts Curriculum: A Booklet for Parents (Spanish Edition) (1991)...	10/5.00*
0-8011-0777-6	The Changing Mathematics Curriculum: A Booklet for Parents (1989)	10/5.00*
0-8011-0891-8	The Changing Mathematics Curriculum: A Booklet for Parents (Spanish Edition) (1991)...	10/5.00*
0-8011-0969-8	Not Schools Alone: Guidelines for Schools and Communities to Prevent the Use of Tobacco, Alcohol, and Other Drugs Among Children and Youth (1991)	3.25
0-8011-0974-4	Parent Involvement Programs in California Public Schools (1991)	6.00

OTHER RECENT PUBLICATIONS

ISBN	Title (Date of publication)	Price
0-8011-0978-7	Course Models for the History–Social Science Framework, Grade Five—United States History and Geography: Making a New Nation (1991)	$7.00
0-8011-0804-7	Foreign Language Framework for California Public Schools (1989)	5.50
0-8011-0712-1	History–Social Science Framework for California Public Schools (1988)	6.00
0-8011-1024-6	It's Elementary! Elementary Grades Task Force Report (1992)	5.00
0-8011-1033-5	Mathematics Framework for California Public Schools, 1992 Edition (1992)	5.50
0-8011-0968-x	Moral and Civic Education and Teaching About Religion (1991 Revised Edition)	3.25
0-8011-0870-5	Science Framework for California Public Schools (1990)	6.50
0-8011-0805-5	Visual and Performing Arts Framework for California Public Schools (1989)	6.00
0-8011-1016-5	With History–Social Science for All: Access for Every Student (1992)	4.25

*Also available in quantities of 100 copies for $30 and 1,000 copies for $230. One copy of each of the three "changing curriculum" booklets in English is available as a set for $3.

ORDERING INFORMATION

Please use the form below or a facsimile to order publications from the California Department of Education. Remittance or purchase order must accompany order. Purchase orders without checks are accepted only from governmental agencies. Stated prices will be in effect until January 1, 1993, and include shipping charges to anywhere in the United States. All sales are final.

A complete list of publications available from the Department, including apprenticeship instructional materials, may be obtained by writing to the address listed below or by calling (916) 445-1260.

To: California Department of Education
Bureau of Publications, Sales Unit
P.O. Box 271
Sacramento, CA 95812-0271

Name _____

Address _____

	City	State	ZIP code

ISBN	Title of publication	Number of copies	Price per copy	Total
				$

Make checks payable to:
California Department of Education

California residents add sales tax.	$
Total amount	$

92 83122   90-92 (003-0006-92, 003-0019-92, & 003-0024-92) 83122, 20073, & 20160 300 10-92 20M